Brexit Revolt: How the UK Left the EU

Michael Mosbacher and Oliver Wiseman

The
New
Culture
Forum

First published in Great Britain in 2016 by
New Culture Forum
55 Tufton St
London
SW1P 3QL

ISBN: 978-1-904863- 68-7

Printed and bound in the United Kingdom

New Culture Forum
55 Tufton St
London
SW1P 3QL
www.newcultureforum.org.uk

Contents

Foreward by Richard Smith   2

Introduction   4

Chapter One: Coming in From the Cold   7

Chapter Two: An In/Out Referendum: From No to Yes   31

Chapter Three: Building the Brexit Coalition   45

Chapter Four: Best of Both Worlds?   67

Chapter Five: "A Six-Week Slagging Match"   81

Chapter Six: Numbers Games   93

Chapter Seven: Breaking Point   107

Chapter Eight: "We Took Back Control!"   119

Appendix: The Results   133

Foreword

The European Union referendum on 23 June 2016 produced a result that the journalist and author Peter Oborne has described as "a revolution as profound as any in our history".

That revolution marked the end of a conflict that formally started in 1972 in Parliament when Prime Minister Edward Heath pushed through the European Communities Act. The 44-year war that followed this great deceit has now concluded, with the British people instructing Parliament to undo the 1972 Act and take the country out of the EU. An episode which was started by Parliament will ultimately be finished by Parliament when it carries out the referendum mandate it cannot possibly ignore.

The campaign and referendum of 2016 were the final chapters in a long and damaging conflict. It was clear to me that Brexit should be documented by the writing of a short contemporary history of events, before the memories of all those involved with this triumph for freedom started to fade. It would also serve to warn off the revisionists within the Establishment who wanted to water down the decision of the British people, in an attempt to sideline the result.

The New Culture Forum and its director, Peter Whittle, have an outstanding track record of producing well-balanced research on contemporary cultural and political subjects. They excelled in bringing to the attention of the public the horrors of Female Genital Mutilation (FGM) and the report An Unpunished Crime strongly influenced policy direction on that issue. Equally incisive works describing the sustained cultural attack on British values from the liberal establishment, research into the impartiality of the BBC and the current state of free speech also come to mind as important contributions to contemporary debate.

To write this account of the EU referendum campaign, Peter commissioned Michael Mosbacher and Oliver Wiseman, who have ploughed through private emails and interviewed figures from across the Eurosceptic movement. The result is a unique insight into the events that led up to the referendum. It demonstrates clearly that the British people, civil society and the Eurosceptic movement got it right. We won.

Richard Smith
Advisory Board
New Culture Forum

Introduction

The United Kingdom will leave the European Union. As we write, much uncertainty surrounds the nature of that exit, its timing and its terms. Yet, in spite of the best efforts of the Remain rump who refuse to accept defeat, anything other than an eventual British departure from the EU seems so unlikely as to not demand serious consideration. That looming departure is the outcome of one of the most remarkable stories in British political history.

The 17,410,742 voters who put a cross next to "Leave" on 23 June 2016 constituted a rag-tag coalition without precedent. Whatever the demographic trends undoubtedly present in the Leave vote, the reasons people voted the way they did were wide-ranging, sometimes even directly contradictory. Their party political preferences were diverse. According to Lord Ashcroft's polling, 58 per cent of Conservative voters at the 2015 general election voted Leave. For Labour, the figure was 37 per cent, for UKIP 96 per cent, for the Liberal Democrats 30 per cent, for the SNP 36 per cent and for the Greens 25 per cent.

Not long ago, the idea that united so eclectic a group of voters on 23 June had been nothing more than the outlandish dream of those at the fringes of British politics. The notion that the country might be better off simply going it alone was something even committed Eurosceptics once only entertained half-seriously. For some, including Conservative MEP Daniel Hannan and UKIP leader Nigel Farage, the EU was the sole cause that motivated them to launch their political careers. But for others just as closely associated with hardline Euroscepticism, the idea that the UK should actually leave was something they would come round to later in the day. Even Conservatives like Bernard Jenkin and Bill Cash, who made a name for themselves as Maastricht rebels in the early 1990s and were willing to be seen by many of their parliamentary colleagues as a fringe nuisance jeopardising effective Tory government over the single issue of Europe, only supported actual departure later. How leaving the EU won the support of a majority of the voters is the story of an outlandish idea coming in from the cold. It is the story of several months of tumultuous campaigning. It is the story of a battle of ideas and egos. It is the story of a Prime Minister who sowed the seeds of his own downfall halfway through his first term. It is the story of how EU leaders spurned the opportunity to demonstrate not only to British people but the people of Europe that they were capable of listening. It is the story of how the Brexiteers nearly let infighting blow their once-in-a-generation opportunity. Above all, it is the story of a democratic revolt, a renunciation of the status quo that marks a fork in the road that will define British politics for years to come.

***

We would like to thank Peter Whittle, Richard Smith and the New Culture Forum for trusting us with the story of the referendum as well as Robert Low, whose editing has been invaluable. Thanks is also due to everyone – too many to name here – who spoke to us and to Daniel Johnson, our editor at Standpoint for his patience while we juggled work at the magazine with writing this book.

We are sure that this account contains sins of omission and commission. These are unavoidable, given the vast amount of information we have digested in so short a time. We have tried our best to keep them to a minimum and to sort fact from fiction in what has been a chaotic year in British politics.

London, September 2016

Margaret Thatcher delivers what came to be known as the Bruges speech to the College of Europe in 1988. She famously warned: "We have not successfully rolled back the frontiers of the state in Britain only to see them re-imposed at a European level".

Picture by: Rebecca Naden/PA Archive/Press Association Images

Chapter One:
Coming in From the cold

The Conservative Party has been at war with itself over Europe for nearly 30 years. Hostilities commenced on 20 September 1988. It remains to be seen if the war ended on 23 June 2016.

The Tories' lows and highs and frequent leadership crises since 1988 have in essence been a conflict about Europe and the UK's relationship with it. Other factors have of course also come into play – but at the core there has been a constant fight about what Britain's relationship with the continent should be. The nature of the Eurosceptic position has changed over time – in the late 1980s no more than a handful of Tory MPs, even behind closed doors, would have supported Brexit. And that of the pro-Europeans has changed too – David Cameron, other than during the referendum campaign itself, would have been seen as a fierce sceptic by the standards of the Thatcher years.

As in any conflict there were skirmishes and warning signs which could have been seen before 20 September 1988 – but Margaret Thatcher's Bruges Speech of that day brought the conflict out into the open. Mrs Thatcher had supported British accession to the European Community under the Heath government in 1973 and as the newly-elected leader of the Conservative Party had campaigned for a Yes vote in support of continued membership in the 1975 referendum. There was a wobble in Mrs Thatcher's relationship with Europe in the early 1980s over her eventually successful demand for a rebate on Britain's contribution to the Community budget, but this was not a profound point of principle.

In 1986 Mrs Thatcher pushed through the ratification of the Single European Act, the first major revision of the treaties establishing the European Community. This extended qualified majority voting to a whole raft of areas of Community policy-making, meaning the UK could be outvoted at European level on many issues for the first time. It also made a commitment to European Monetary Union at a future point. Mrs Thatcher's rationale was that this extension of European Community powers was necessary to create and implement a single European market, of which she was a strong advocate. In her view, talk of European Monetary Union was simply that – talk. But the Single European Act undoubtedly amounted to a substantial diminution of British sovereignty.

The Bruges speech – to the College of Europe – reads today like a rather mild attack on further European integration. Mrs Thatcher said: "Britain does not dream of some cosy, isolated existence on the fringes of the European Community. Our destiny is in Europe, as part of the Community." But she also said: "My first guiding principle is this: willing and active cooperation between independent sovereign states is the best way to build a successful European Community . . . Let Europe be a family of nations, understanding each other better, appreciating each other more, doing more together but relishing our national identity no less than our common European endeavour."

This vision was radically at odds with that of Jacques Delors, the French socialist who was President of the European Commission from 1985 to 1994 and who was instrumental in pushing forward a Euro-federalist agenda. Delors had addressed the TUC Conference in Bournemouth earlier that September. The Labour Party – and the British labour movement more widely – had been hostile to the European project during much of the 1980s. The 1983 Labour manifesto stated: "The next Labour government, committed to radical, socialist policies for reviving the British economy, is bound to find continued membership a most serious obstacle to the fulfilment of those policies . . . British withdrawal from the Community is the right policy for Britain, to be completed well within the lifetime of the parliament. That is our commitment."

In 1986 Labour MPs opposed the implementation of the Single European Act. The irony is that in 1986 future sceptics such as the Conservative MP George Gardiner, who would go on to defect to the Referendum Party, and Norman Tebbit, arch-Brexiteer-to-be, supported this major step towards further European integration, while Tony Blair and Gordon Brown voted against it. Bill Cash, later the leader of the Maastricht revolt, put down an amendment to underscore the primacy of Parliament over EC law but this was not selected for debate despite his best endeavours – and he then voted with the government. There were only a handful of Tories who opposed this integrationist move as a whole: Jonathan Aitken, Nick Budgen, Edward Du Cann, Neil Hamilton (now a UKIP member of the Welsh Assembly), Roger Moate, Harvey Proctor and Teddy Taylor. Some others did abstain.

Labour had gradually been edging away from its Eurosceptic stance, and

Delors went to address the TUC to solidify this. His pitch was that the Labour movement could gain through Europe what it had lost with Mrs Thatcher's reforms – in fact, that through Europe it could gain trade union entrenchment, employment protection and social rights on a level it had only previously dreamed of. Delors' speech brought about – or at the very least consolidated – a dramatic change in the Labour movement's attitude towards European integration.

Mrs Thatcher's Bruges speech must be seen against this background. Its most famous passage – "We have not successfully rolled back the frontiers of the state in Britain, only to see them reimposed at a European level with a European super-state exercising a new dominance from Brussels" – is a direct response to this Delors-ist, and increasingly British Labour movement agenda. As one Conservative MP of the era put it to us, "The Delors speech is when Thatcher got it." In some ways, Delors was thus the progenitor of contemporary British Euroscepticism.

Delors became a hate figure for the Eurosceptic British press. The Sun ran one of its most famous headlines – *Up Yours Delors* – on 2 November 1990. The story urged all Sun readers to turn in the direction of France at noon on that day and shout out what Delors could do with his idea of a single currency. At a slightly more elevated level, Boris Johnson, aged 24, became Brussels correspondent for the Daily Telegraph in 1989 and started to feed its readers a regular diet of horror stories about the Delors Commission and its meddling in Britain's affairs.

One aspect of the tabloids' European Community bashing in the late 1980s and early 1990s were frequent claims – similar to those made in a 1990 Spectator interview by Nicholas Ridley, who had to resign from Mrs Thatcher's cabinet as a result – that it was all a German-run racket. What the Germans had tried to do in two world wars they were now achieving via Brussels – or so this crude line of attack went. It is clearly a line that resonated strongly with Mrs Thatcher's own attitudes to Germany. Interestingly it is one line of attack which has all but entirely disappeared from the debate today in the UK, although it lives on in critical commentary about the EU from other parts of Europe, especially Greece, Italy and Poland.

Some of the issues raised in the Bruges speech still have echoes in today's debates. There was much about the role of Nato and its central place in maintaining peace in Europe, rather than – by implication – that of the European Community. There was also mention of the need to maintain border controls "to stop the movement of . . . terrorists and illegal immigrants". There are other passages that would be unthinkable from any other contemporary politician: "The story of how Europeans explored and colonised – and yes, without apology – civilised much of the world is an extraordinary tale of talent, skill and courage."

In February 1989 Patrick Robertson, a 20-year-old history student at Keble College, Oxford, dropped out of university to set up the Bruges Group, with the encouragement of Ralph Harris, the proto-Thatcherite founding Director of the free-market Institute of Economic Affairs, who had been ennobled by Mrs Thatcher. This was the first of the new wave of Eurosceptic pressure groups and arguably marks the start of the contemporary Eurosceptic movement in the UK. The Bruges Group modelled itself on the pro-market think tanks and had an advisory board of academics; just like the think tanks, it intended to keep politicians at one remove. It would publish pamphlets and reports and hold meetings and conferences. Boris Johnson was a favourite and frequent speaker. A separate purely parliamentary group, Friends of the Bruges Group, was established by Bill Cash. Its aim was to pull the Conservative Party in a more Eurosceptic direction. Up to 130 MPs came to be associated with it in one way or another.

Older organisations such as the Anti-Common Market League and the Campaign for an Independent Britain still existed but had become rather geriatric and moribund. Daniel Hannan, a Conservative Member of the European Parliament who was a leading figure in calling for an In-Out referendum and who then campaigned for Brexit, discussed with the authors the state of Euroscepticism pre-Bruges: "[The 1975 referendum] was a two-to-one defeat and everyone accepted the result, and with the blip of the Michael Foot [Labour] 1983 election manifesto there was no Eurosceptic movement for the next 15 years in Britain really. Of course, there were a few old-stagers, including [businessman and Labour donor] John Mills making the argument but nobody was listening. There was Teddy Taylor. It was a cause like Esperanto or naturism. It just wasn't serious, it wasn't real. That began to change, first with the Bruges speech and then with the Delors rush towards political and monetary union at the end of the 1980s."

In December 1989 Mrs Thatcher was challenged for the Conservative leadership by Sir Anthony Meyer, a strongly Europhile MP. Meyer was never a serious candidate – and received the votes of only 33 Tory MPs against Mrs Thatcher's 314, with 27 spoilt ballots and abstentions – but he was putting down a marker to show the disquiet that Europhile Tories were feeling about the Prime Minister's growing Euroscepticism. The following November Mrs Thatcher was forced out of office after being challenged for the leadership by Michael Heseltine. This is not the place to revisit that leadership battle. The reasons for her removal were not solely about Europe – other factors came into pay, such as her leadership style, the unpopularity of the poll tax and the growing fear among Tory MPs that they would lose the next election. Nevertheless, Europe was the most important single issue which brought Margaret Thatcher down. This is certainly the view of many of the Tory MPs who would later play a key role in pushing for a referendum and then supporting Brexit.

More specifically, by 1990 it was clear that the European Community was heading towards major treaty change. This would decisively put Europe on a federalist trajectory and abandon the notion – if it was ever a valid one – of it being an alliance of sovereign, independent states freely cooperating when they saw fit on areas of common interest and mutual benefit. Mrs Thatcher – or so it is now widely believed by Eurosceptic Tory MPs – would not have gone along with such a treaty and would thus have been the major impediment to European integration. From their perspective, she was removed from office by Conservative supporters of the European project to enable further integration.

The treaty which came about was Maastricht, and it was during the battles over its ratification that demands for a European referendum became a live issue in UK politics for the first time since 1975. Negotiations for the treaty were successfully concluded by European governments in December 1991 and the treaty was signed on 7 February 1992. At first the negotiating stance of John Major's government was widely praised. There was an advisory vote in the House of Commons on 19 December 1991. Perhaps for the sake of party unity, Mrs Thatcher merely abstained. She would make her feelings rather clearer later on.

The treaty transformed the Community into the European Union. It created a common EU citizenship and extended the Union's remit to foreign and security policy. The treaty also created the framework for establishing a single currency and obligated members to join provided they met certain economic convergence criteria – but Britain negotiated for itself an opt-out from this so it could decide whether to join the euro at a later date. The UK also had an opt-out from the Social Chapter of the treaty, covering employment law, but this was subsequently given up by the Blair government.

The real fight over Maastricht, however, had to wait until after the 1992 general election. Parliament was dissolved on 16 March and the Conservatives won their unexpected majority of 21 on 9 April.

The Maastricht Treaty led to the formation of a new party to challenge the Tories from a Eurosceptic direction – or rather by standing against them to persuade them to become more Eurosceptic. Alan Sked, an acerbic and eloquent historian at the London School of Economics, a specialist on the decline of the Habsburg Empire who had been a doctoral student of A.J.P. Taylor, had been an active member of the Liberal Party, for which he stood as a parliamentary candidate in the 1970 general election. He was involved in and wrote for the Bruges Group from its inception. He had, however, come to feel that more than pamphleteering was needed to make the case against further integration and to punish the Tories for their wayward course.

Sked founded the Anti-Federalist League in 1991. He was assisted in this endeavour by Helen Szamuely, an argumentative fellow alumnus of A.J.P. Taylor and daughter of Hungarian and Russian communists turned anti-communist exiles. Her great-uncle, Tibor Szamuely, was Hungary's Trotsky in its short-lived revolutionary government of 1919. He came to a violent end, either killing himself when he knew the game was up or being murdered for his efforts. In Martin Amis's book on the British Left and Stalin, *Koba The Dread*, he recalls "making a cordially unrequited pass at Helen Szamuely" on the day of his Oxford viva in 1972, and then passing out. Since her Anti-Federalist days, Szamuely has passed through and worked for virtually every Eurosceptic organisation.

The League's name was a conscious homage to Richard Cobden and John Bright's Anti-Corn Law League, founded in 1838 to oppose protectionism, and which, among many other activities, put up parliamentary candidates against prominent protectionists. The Corn Laws were repealed by Robert Peel's ministry in 1846. Sked has said of the Anti-Federalist League: "I thought it would be the equivalent of the Anti-Corn Law League. Just as the Anti-Corn Law League converted Peel to free trade, the Anti-Federalist League would convert the Tory party to Euroscepticism and to British independence."

Sked was thrown out of the Bruges Group for putting up candidates against the Tories. At the same public meeting in which the Bruges Group's then chairman, fellow LSE academic and conservative political philosopher Kenneth Minogue, announced that Sked was "standing down" from the group – much to Sked's surprise and annoyance – the 28-year-old Nigel Farage first met Sked. Farage joined the League and started out on his European adventure.

The Anti-Federalist League's first electoral outing in the 1992 election was not exactly a resounding success. They fielded 17 candidates, all of whom lost their deposit with varying degrees of ease. Sked stood in Bath against Chris Patten, then Chairman of the Conservative Party and in charge of its election campaign; he was a particular bête noire of Eurosceptics both for his policy stances and his role in the removal of Mrs Thatcher. Sked got 117 votes, Patten 21,950. Patten nevertheless lost his seat to the Liberal Democrats and was given the Governorship of Hong Kong by Major as a consolation prize. Despite the disparity in votes, Sked claims that he was responsible for Patten losing his seat. At a constituency hustings he pressed Patten to apologise for the poll tax, the introduction of which he had personally overseen as Environment Secretary under Mrs Thatcher. Patten first prevaricated, then refused to apologise. In Sked's analysis, the resulting publicity cost Patten the seat.

Other Anti-Federalist results were equally uninspiring. Helen Szamuely received 41 votes in Hammersmth, and this was fairly typical. By far the League's best result of the night was in Staffordshire Moorlands, where its candidate received 2,121 votes – 3.4 per cent. Only one other candidate – in Leominster – got more than one per cent of the vote. Sked stood in two by-elections early in the new parliament – in Newbury and Christchurch, both in the summer of 1993. He outperformed his Bath result but still only obtained just over one per cent of the vote in each. The by-elections were better remembered for the Liberal Democrats overturning previously impregnable Conservative majorities. Nevertheless, Sked received much more publicity than the League's poor results might suggest. He was a good media performer and with his academic and liberal credentials could not easily be dismissed as a crank.

Sked realised that the Anti-Federalist League was not a name that resonated with the electorate. Furthermore, some who heard its name thought not so much of the Anti-Corn Law League as of a rather less worthy political organisation, the League of Empire Loyalists. This latter organisation operated on the fringes of the Conservative Party in the late 1950s and early 1960s, disrupting Tory party conferences with stunts and shouts of "Macmillan is a traitor". They were not just Empire nostalgists but altogether less savoury. The group was set up by an erstwhile British Union of Fascists member, A.K. Chesterton (cousin of the author G.K. Chesterton) who was convinced that the dissolution of empire was a Jewish plot. It became one of the founding bodies of the National Front, with A.K. Chesterton serving as its first chairman. Any link with the League of Empire Loyalists was particularly unfortunate as Sked had done his very best to avoid any association with the far Right. Indeed, anyone who had ever been a member of a far-right organisation was banned from joining or standing for the Anti-Federalist League. A name change for the latter-day League was thus in order – and in September 1993 the Anti-Federalist League became the United Kingdom Independence Party.

Sked remained as leader of UKIP until after the 1997 general election. It is hard to imagine a figure more at variance with today's image of a UKIP supporter than Sked – a Scottish cosmopolitan university academic, who speaks and writes in German, French, Italian and Hungarian.

After the 1992 election the real battle over Maastricht moved to the Commons. The rebellion of 1992-93 by Conservative MPs – led by Bill Cash – over the ratification of Maastricht was undoubtedly the most serious, vicious and prolonged revolt against any governing party by a group of its own MPs since 1945. Subsequent rebellions on Europe – such as the one against Cameron on holding an In/Out referendum before this became government policy – were larger but they were certainly not as lengthy or bitter.

The rebellion really took off after Danish voters – in a referendum mandated by their constitution on 2 June 1992 – narrowly rejected the Maastricht Treaty. The rebels put forward a stack of amendments to the legislation. In the process of its ratification, Bill Cash voted against the government and defied the whip on 52 occasions, Teddy Taylor on 53. A total of 50 Conservative MPs voted against the whip in at least one division. The rebels were well-organised and ran their own whipping operation.

In the largest single rebellion – on the final reading of the Bill – 41 Tories voted against the government. But as Philip Cowley, the doyen of academic observers of parliamentary rebellions, observes, "What was surprising about the rebellions [...] was not how many MPs rebelled but – given the depth of hostility to the treaty within the Conservative parliamentary party – how few."

Many prominent later Brexiteers played a significant role in pushing the ratification of the Maastricht Treaty through the Commons. David Davis – later a hard-line Leaver and now the Minister for Brexit – was a government whip; Peter Lilley and Michael Howard were in the cabinet; John Redwood – who in 1995 stood against John Major for the leadership of the Conservative Party on a strongly Eurosceptic although still far from Brexit platform – was a government minister.

The Danish referendum result also meant that calls for a European referendum became prominent in the UK for the first time since 1975. If Denmark could have a referendum on the treaty, along with France, Ireland and Italy – in a mirror image of the Danish result, France narrowly approved it, by 51 to 49 per cent, while Ireland and Italy produced strong Yes votes – why could Britain not have one too? Bill Cash launched the all-party Maastricht Referendum Campaign to build public pressure. After the Danish and French results, Eurosceptics were convinced that they would win a referendum on the treaty – if only they could get one. At this stage hardly anyone was calling for a referendum on EC membership – indeed most of the Maastricht rebels would publicly declare that they supported it.

The fight over Maastricht poisoned relations within the parliamentary Conservative party for at least the rest of that parliament and contributed to the atmosphere of decay which led to the Tories' cataclysmic defeat in 1997, notwithstanding the fact that Tony Blair as Labour leader would have made matters difficult for any Conservative government.

In November 1994 eight Tory MPs lost the party's whip over their refusal to back the government on a European finance measure – and a ninth, Sir Richard Body, resigned the Tory whip in sympathy with them. The whip was restored to the eight in April 1995; Body remained whipless until 1996.

This first launched the recurrent speculation in Conservative politics of whether this or that MP might join UKIP or indeed at that stage some other Eurosceptic formation outside the Tory Party. Indeed, of the whipless nine, three did join UKIP after leaving parliament – Christopher Gill, Theresa Gorman and Sir Richard Body.

Then a billionaire came along to put his money behind the referendum cause – and this at a time when billionaires were rarer than they are today. Sir James Goldsmith had been the quintessential corporate raider, the asset stripper par excellence (although he did not like the term and preferred "debundler") of the 1960s, '70s and '80s. He had been regular fodder for the British press – and, notoriously, *Private Eye* – for his wealth, wives, mistresses, and right-wing politics. He was also a passionate environmentalist – his elder brother Teddy Goldsmith was in many ways the founder of the British green movement and set up *The Ecologist* magazine.

Goldsmith withdrew from many of his businesses in the late 1980s. He had come to see globalisation as a threat and advocated protectionist economic policies. For a Eurosceptic his position was slightly odd in that he supported free trade within Europe – and indeed other trading blocs – but not globally. In France he published a book of his thoughts on trade and the future of Europe which was a bestseller. In the summer of 1994 Goldsmith had been elected in France to the European Parliament as the second-placed candidate on Philippe de Villiers' L'Autre Europe list, which was both Eurosceptic and protectionist.

Goldsmith had long been a supporter of UK think tanks. He was an early donor to the Bruges Group and funded Bill Cash's push for a Maastricht referendum. But he felt that this was not enough. In late 1994 the Referendum Party was launched – founded, funded and led by Goldsmith.

Goldsmith's entry into British electoral politics was on the single issue of holding a referendum on Britain's relations with the EU. The Referendum Party – to which Goldsmith pledged £40 million – proposed running a candidate in every seat in which the main party candidates did not support holding a referendum. It was Goldsmith's view that once the Referendum Party had won an election and held its referendum – and once the UK had regained its sovereignty – the party would dissolve and another general election would be called.

The party's referendum would not quite be on an In/Out question, but it came very close. The proposed question was, "Do you want the United Kingdom to be part of a federal Europe or do you want the United Kingdom to return to an association of sovereign nations that are part of a common trading market?"

Patrick Robertson moved from the Bruges Group to run the Referendum Party for Goldsmith. Priti Patel – later one of the Conservative minsters who supported Brexit in 2016 – was the party's head of press. George Eustice, now Conservative MP for Camborne and Redruth and an agriculture minister who supported Brexit, also worked for the party. Others who worked for it and would play a later role in the Brexit debate include Marc Henri Glendenning of the People's Pledge and Douglas Smith, David Cameron's speechwriter.

The Referendum Party stood in 547 seats in the 1997 general election and received 812,000 votes – an average of 3 per cent in the seats in which it stood: not a bad result for a start-up party, but less good if one considers how much it spent. Not only did it run a massive advertising campaign, it also distributed – how quaint it now seems – more than five million video tapes to UK households. UKIP put up 193 candidates – often running against the Referendum Party – and received 106,000 votes, an eighth of the Referendum Party's vote but after spending much less than a hundredth of the larger party's outlay. Sked claims he was very keen to come to an agreement with the Referendum Party but that Robertson, who opposed cooperation, stopped him making his case directly to Goldsmith. This would not be the last time we would see Eurosceptic campaigns competing against each other.

The Referendum Party had big plans for continuing after 1997, but Goldsmith died less than three months after the general election. Unbeknownst to the public, he had been terminally ill with pancreatic cancer during the election campaign. His party became the non-electioneering Democracy Movement, which was eventually in 2011 the progenitor of the People's Pledge – a group that played a role in convincing David Cameron to support an In/Out referendum.

The Eurosceptic parties were obviously not the main event of the 1997 general election. Their results were overshadowed by Tony Blair winning a majority of 179 and forming the first Labour government in 18 years. The big European issue which was fast coming up on the horizon was the launch of the common currency, the euro. Britain had secured its opt-out, but the euro would come into existence on 1 January 1999: the participating countries now had a single, common monetary policy, while their currencies ceased to exist independently and had a fixed, permanent rate of exchange against each other. National currencies in the form of notes and coins would disappear and be replaced by the euro in early 2002.

In its final years Major's cabinet had become irreconcilably divided on whether or not to join the euro, with Michael Heseltine and Kenneth Clarke strongly supportive and Michael Portillo, Peter Lilley, William Hague and Michael Howard equally adamantly against. Major's solution was to sideline the issue by promising to hold a referendum before Britain joined. To stop the Tories from turning the euro and their pledge of a referendum into an election issue, Labour matched that promise in its 1997 manifesto. Britain would thus not join the euro without a referendum. The timing meant it was extremely unlikely that Britain would join the single currency when it launched, but membership remained a live issue. Blair was a convinced and committed supporter, and would do everything he could to make Britain join during his premiership.

David Owen, the former Labour Foreign Secretary who was one of the Gang of Four that founded the Social Democratic Party in 1981 and who served as its leader from 1983, recounted to us how he had a meeting with Blair in 1996 in which Blair tried to persuade him to rejoin the Labour Party. Blair thought it would be a big boost to Labour if some of the leading figures who had left it over the party's leftward drift in the early 1980s would rejoin before the coming general election. All was going well in Owen's discussion with Blair until they reached the topic of the euro. It became clear that Blair was an adamant supporter, while Owen opposed the whole project. Indeed it was Owen's view even then that the problem with the euro was not just British membership but that the project was dangerous per se and would be extremely damaging to the whole of Europe, Britain included, whether we were members or not. Blair's support for the euro was an insurmountable block to Owen rejoining Labour. Unlike his colleagues on the Labour centre-right of the 1970s and then in the SDP, Owen had always been much more sceptical both of European integration and the benefits of mass migration. Labour's growing opposition to the European Community was not for Owen – unlike for nearly all of his colleagues – one of the reasons for his split from Labour.

In 1997 Chancellor Gordon Brown announced his five economic tests which had to be met before the Labour government would support joining the euro. Only if the government felt they had been met would a referendum be held and a Yes vote recommended. It is now known that the five tests were dreamed up by Brown and his then economic adviser Ed Balls, allegedly in the back of a taxi while on a visit to New York, with the specific aim of at least delaying any decision indefinitely, if not stopping British membership. This was not, however, known at the time: many people feared the economic tests were so vague that an argument could be made at any point as to whether or not they had been met or looked like being met. While it is now clear that Balls opposed joining the euro on principle, it is still not known if Brown only opposed membership because Blair supported it.

Membership of the euro thus became the battleground over European policy in Britain in the late 1990s and early 2000s. In the Conservative leadership election following their 1997 defeat, the early front-runner Ken Clarke, despite being much more experienced and better-known, eventually lost to William Hague largely because of his support for European integration in general, and euro membership in particular. Being out of step with so many of his fellow Conservatives on Europe cost Clarke the party's leadership not just in 1997 but also in 2001. With hindsight, indeed, what seems bizarre is how close Clarke came to becoming leader when he was so at odds with the direction of travel on Europe of the vast bulk of his party – Clarke remains as Europhile a British politician as one will find outside the ranks of the Liberal Democrats.

With the election of Hague, the Tories took a stance of resolute and principled opposition to joining the euro and ran in the 2001 general election on a platform of opposing the single currency. Indeed "Save the Pound" was the main theme of the last days of that year's Conservative election campaign – the election in which David Cameron was first elected to the Commons.

In 1998 Rodney Leach, alongside Stanley Kalms, then chairman of Dixons, founded Business for Sterling to campaign against Britain joining the euro. Leach was an establishment figure, a merchant banker who was the leading non-family figure at Jardine Matheson, the Keswick family's vast Hong Kong and Far East trading conglomerate. He became a convinced opponent of European integration when his second wife, Jessica Douglas-Home – widow of the Thatcherite former editor of *The Times* Charles Douglas-Home – persuaded him to read the Maastricht Treaty. It convinced him that the European Union was "a bureaucratic oligarchy, not a democracy". Although having a low public profile, Leach – who was made a Conservative life peer in 2006 – would remain a major player in organising and fundraising for various campaigns against further European integration until his death just before the referendum in 2016.

The logic behind making the anti-euro campaign initially a business-based campaign was that those campaigning for British euro membership argued that it was business which needed Britain to join. Euro membership, or so they argued, was what British business needed to prosper and compete. Indeed the CBI, representing the UK's largest firms, was perhaps the most vocal voice in favour of joining the euro, or at least of doing so when the time was right.

Business for Sterling came together with New Europe – a cross-party organisation set up by David Owen to campaign against membership of the euro while explicitly supporting continued membership of EU – to set up the No campaign in 2000. This was to be the campaign for a No vote in a referendum on the euro that both Business for Sterling and New Europe then feared Blair would call on the back of the bounce he would receive from winning a second general election, likely to be held in 2001. The No campaigns slogan was, "Europe Yes, Euro No". It is worth noting that Owen and former Chancellor Nigel Lawson – another leading figure in New Europe and a strong and longstanding opponent of British membership of the euro, who had warned Mrs Thatcher in 1986 of the dangers of a single currency, as first mooted in the Single European Act – were at that stage still supporters of British membership of the European Union. They would both come to be prominent supporters of Brexit campaigners in 2016.

The pro-euro side was also organising and had set up its referendum vehicle, Britain in Europe. It was launched by Blair, Clarke and Heseltine in 1999. Clarke and Heseltine soon became critical of Blair for not making the case for euro membership stridently enough. At the time they were unaware of the extent of Gordon Brown's opposition.

An early referendum in the UK, if it was on the cards, was derailed by a vote in Denmark. That country was the only other EU member to have a formal opt-out from the single currency. This was given to it alongside an opt-out from EU citizenship and two other areas as a successful sop to change its mind after rejecting Maastricht in 1992; the Danes accepted the treaty with these concessions in 1993. But a referendum in Denmark in

September 2000 unexpectedly rejected euro membership by 53 to 47 per cent. When the referendum was called the pro-euro side was leading and the Danish commentariat was predicting a clear Yes vote. In the UK no poll had shown a majority for euro membership – the best polls for the pro-euro lobby showed support for joining at just over 40 per cent. The Danish result reduced the appetite for a British referendum, quite apart from Brown's opposition. After the 9/11 terror attacks in 2001 Blair had other priorities and a referendum slipped further down the government's agenda.

Many of those who would later play a leading role in the Brexit referendum worked for Business for Sterling. Nick Herbert was its first Chief Executive. He would leave in 2000 to set up the think tank Reform, which aimed to introduce market-based reforms in healthcare, schooling and the public services. In 2005 he was elected Conservative MP for Arundel and South Downs. Much to the surprise of many people given his Eurosceptic pedigree, he came to be a prominent campaigner for Remain in 2016. For the Brexit referendum Herbert would set up Conservatives for Reform in Europe, a group of Conservative MPs who saw themselves as Eurosceptics – and many of whom had a long history of campaigning against European integration – but would nevertheless campaign for continued membership of the EU.

Dominic Cummings – in 2016 the strategist for Vote Leave – also worked for Business for Sterling. Initially he was appointed, aged 27, as campaign director and later became Chief Executive. Cummings is credited with bringing Harry Enfield and Bob Geldof on board with the anti-euro campaign – a tactic which would not work in 2016 when Geldof was a notably aggressive Remainer. Some have mischievously come to the conclusion that Herbert supported Remain in 2016 as he could not bear to again work alongside Cummings after his less than happy experiences on the anti-euro campaign. George Eustice – earlier of the Referendum Party, a UKIP candidate in the 1999 European elections, later a pro-Brexit minister – took over as Chief Executive after Cummings left in 2002 to become Head of Strategy for the Conservative Party, where he lasted for just eight months.

The last point at which a UK referendum on euro membership seemed possible was in 2003. Owen recalls the real fear of the No campaigners that a referendum would be called – how improbable it now seems – on the back of a Baghdad bounce for Blair after victory in Iraq. The Prime Minister would then have been in a position to tell Brown that he would have to support euro membership or resign. In Owen's view Brown would probably have backed euro membership under those circumstances, although Balls never would.

It was not to be. In June 2003 Brown announced that a review of the evidence showed four of his five economic tests had not yet been met but that progress would be reviewed for the 2004 Budget. During that Budget speech Brown ruled out another assessment of the tests in 2004, but held out the possibility of it happening in 2005, the likely year of the next general election. This was seen as kicking the issue into the long grass by the campaigners on each side. Both of the proto-referendum campaigns closed up shop.

Cummings and others in the No campaign came to believe that it was their brilliantly effective strategy that won the battle over euro membership. Indeed they thought the fact that no referendum was held illustrated just how well their strategy had worked, and why they believed 12 years later that much of what they had done then could be used in the Brexit referendum.

Yet at least as convincing an explanation of what happened with the euro is that Blair had a Chancellor who, for whatever reason, was adamant that the UK would not join the common currency – and the Prime Minister was never sufficiently powerful, or had sufficient guts, to sideline Brown. If that is the real story – and it does now seem convincing – it means that the activities of Business for Sterling were a mere sideshow, albeit perhaps an important one for creating the mood music.

UKIP had made its first breakthrough in the 1999 elections to the European Parliament. The Blair government – as part of its attempt in its early days to create a centre-left realignment of British politics and bring the Liberal Democrats into the family – wanted to show that it was open to proportional representation, and so changed the electoral system for European elections to a form of PR. Previously, European elections in Great Britain had been via first past the post, with 84 large constituencies each returning one member. This was replaced by nine regions of varying sizes for England and one each for Wales and Scotland – Northern Ireland already had a different electoral system for European elections and this was unchanged – where the parties would put forward lists of candidates.

Voters would choose between the lists – they could not select a preference for a particular candidate within the list, the parties themselves ranked the candidates – and the seats for the region would be allocated proportionately.

Under the old system it was very difficult for smaller parties to win any seats – indeed the 1994 European elections were the first time the Liberal Democrats or their predecessor parties won seats, and they won only two. UKIP had stood in those elections under Sked on a platform of not taking up its seats if elected as it regarded the European Parliament as illegitimate: a rather academic point as it stood no chance of winning any seats. It received 150,000 votes, about one per cent.

In 1999 UKIP obtained nearly 700,000 votes, seven per cent of those who voted in a low turnout election: under a quarter of the electorate went to the polls. This was enough under the new electoral system to elect three MEPs – one of whom, for the South East region, was Nigel Farage, now 35. A fellow new South East region MEP, but for the Conservatives, was 27-year-old Daniel Hannan.

UKIP's new leader, Michael Holmes, had reversed Sked's abstentionist policy. Thus Farage went off to Brussels, along with Holmes from the South West and, from the Eastern Region, funeral director Jeffrey Titford, who had been the Referendum Party's most successful candidate in 1997. He had gained more than nine per cent of the vote in Harwich, the seat for which UKIP's only current MP, Douglas Carswell, was first elected as a Conservative and part of which is now in his present constituency of Clacton.

This breakthrough – as Sked has pointed out to us – is more important than it might at first seem, since it meant that UKIP had an institutional foothold, access to European Parliament funds and a career trajectory for aspiring politicians. Without this it would have been much more difficult to keep activists on board and to build a party. Indeed, without it UKIP might very well not have survived. The European Parliament played an unwitting but leading role in making UKIP the force it became.

The 1999 European elections were won – against all expectations – by the Conservatives, who had run a Brussels-bashing, Eurosceptic campaign. The lesson that Hague drew from this was that banging on about Europe was what won Tories elections. It is why he put saving the pound at the heart of the Tories' 2001 general election campaign – with rather less success.

There was one striking difference between UKIP's European election campaign in 1999 and its subsequent campaigns – in 1999 immigration played no role. As Farage put it to us, "Not only not an issue, the word did not appear in my election literature. How about that? I've checked that in the last few months. I did not mention it once. Then we had free movement between countries of comparable wealth, education and healthcare systems."

This all changed with the accession to the EU of eight Central and Eastern European countries, along with Cyprus and Malta, on 1 May 2004. While existing EU members could not restrict free movement from the accession states, they could impose certain temporary controls on the right to work on nationals from the new members. The Blair government chose not to apply any restrictions. The official government prediction was that post-accession, to give one example, 15,000 Poles would settle in the UK each year. In fact by 2007 more than 500,000 Poles had arrived in the UK.

The 2004 European elections were held just a month after the new members had joined. Farage says that this is when it first became an issue: "In 2004 we saw the first set of European elections with eight or [from 2007] ten former communist countries and that was the first election we campaigned on immigration. We made a very big call, which was that it would lead to huge numbers, and we were proved right."

In 2004 UKIP received a huge boost by recruiting Robert Kilroy-Silk, former Labour MP and then presenter of a daily morning TV show for 17 years, as a European election candidate. Kilroy-Silk's show had been axed by the BBC because of a column by him in the *Sunday Express* which asked of the Arab world, "Apart from oil – which was discovered, is produced and is paid for by the West – what do they contribute? [Should we] admire them for being suicide bombers, limb-amputators, women repressors?" Less probably, Kilroy-Silk had been a lecturer in politics at the University of Liverpool before embarking on his first, Labour political career. While he was an undergraduate at the LSE he was taught by future Bruges Group chairman Kenneth Minogue, who thought he was one of the five or six brightest students he had taught throughout his 40-year academic career.

The combination of fear of looming large-scale migration and Kilroy-

Silk turbocharged UKIP's support in the 2004 election. They came in third, beating the Liberal Democrats and obtaining 16 per cent of the vote and 12 seats. Kilroy-Silk rapidly fell out with UKIP, but the mass migration the party had predicted became a reality. In the 2009 European elections, UKIP's support saw a modest increase: the party gained one extra seat, but thanks to a steep fall in Labour support, it came second. European elections were also occasions when prominent Tories were thrown out of the party for calling on the electorate to vote for UKIP. In 2004 three Tory members of the House of Lords, including Malcolm Pearson, who would join UKIP in 2007 and later serve as its leader, were expelled; in 2009 they were followed by Tory peer and former party treasurer Stanley Kalms and Stuart Wheeler, who had given the Tories their largest ever single donation of £5 million in 2001.

After the non-event of the euro referendum, the Blair years would have one more non-referendum. In 2001 the EU embarked on the three-year process of drawing up a constitution to replace its existing plethora of treaties with a single all-encompassing agreement. A campaign for a referendum was launched with the support of Leach and Kalms – but Blair consistently rejected this, arguing that there was no need for a referendum as the constitution would merely codify existing treaties and arrangements. To general surprise Blair changed his line and in April 2004 announced that the UK would have a referendum on the constitution. This was a high-risk strategy: every single poll on the issue suggested that British voters would reject it

Why Blair changed his position is not clear, although there has been speculation that he agreed to this concession in order to keep the Murdoch newspapers on board for Labour in the 2005 general election. The referendum was expected to be in 2006 – and the 2005 election manifestos of the three main parties all pledged to hold it

Kalms and Leach brought in Cummings to set up and run the No campaign. In a reprise of the campaign against the euro he came up with the not entirely original slogan, "Europe Yes, Constitution No". The belief was that this campaign would really get going after the 2005 general election.

Labour were reelected – with a much reduced majority – in May. Later that same month a referendum in France rejected the constitution by 55 per cent to 45 per cent. The French rejection was followed on 1 June by a

No vote of more than 60 per cent in the Netherlands. The constitution was dead – and a few days later the British referendum was cancelled.

The EU would not, however, leave the matter there and much of the constitution's content was revived with the 2007 Treaty of Lisbon. By now Brown had become Prime Minister and his government argued that it was not bound by the Labour Party's manifesto commitment to hold a referendum on the constitution as the treaty was different. David Cameron's Tories took the opposite line and strongly pushed for a referendum.

It should be remembered that when Cameron was elected leader of the Conservative Party in 2005 he had made a big pitch for the votes of Eurosceptic Tory MPs – and underlined his own Eurosceptic credentials – by pledging to take the Tories out of the federalist European Peoples Party/European Democrats group in the European Parliament and attempt to set up a new Eurosceptic grouping. It was a pledge that the early leadership front-runner David Davis would not match. While Davis was by most standards the more Eurosceptic candidate, some of his more hard-line colleagues were still suspicious of him because of his role as a whip during Maastricht, and his failure to make the same commitment as Cameron did not help.

MEPs in the European Parliament sit in cross-national, broadly ideological groupings, such as the Party of European Socialists for the mainstream centre-left and the Alliance of Liberals and Democrats for centrist parties. The group the Conservatives were members of – the EPP/ED, the European Democrats – represents European Christian Democratic parties and is arguably the single most pro-integrationist in the entire parliament. This might seem like a deeply esoteric issue but it mattered greatly to some Tory MPs and even more so to Eurosceptic MEPs, most notably Daniel Hannan. The move won over an important block of MPs: it is, for example, why the newly-elected Douglas Carswell, who would defect to UKIP in 2014, voted for Cameron in 2005. They took their time, but in 2009 the Conservatives –¬ with a great deal of effort from Hannan – did manage to set up a new, respectable Eurosceptic grouping in the European Parliament, the European Conservatives and Reformists.

The Lisbon Treaty was ratified by the British parliament in June 2008 but it would not come into force until it had been ratified by all the EU's member states. Cameron continued to call for a referendum until this process was concluded and the treaty had come into force. Ireland was the only country to hold a referendum on the treaty's ratification – and rejected it in June 2008. After some minor concessions, Ireland overturned the result with a second referendum in October 2009. Vaclav Klaus, then President of the Czech Republic, was a strong Eurosceptic and adamantly opposed to the treaty. He did his very best to stop ratification, trying every delaying tactic he could, but eventually these ran out. Cameron wrote to Klaus in October 2009 to urge him to delay signing the treaty until after the UK general election which would have to be held by May 2010 – and then an incoming Conservative government could hold a referendum. But Klaus had no more cards to play and the Czech Republic ratified the treaty in November 2009.

At this stage Cameron changed his position and argued that, since the treaty would now come into force, it was too late for the UK to hold a referendum. A referendum on the treaty after it had come into force would be perilously close to an In/Out vote, something Cameron wanted to avoid. Instead, the Tories pledged that there would be a referendum over any future treaty. Nevertheless, many Eurosceptics regarded this as a betrayal

Malcolm Pearson, who became leader of UKIP in November 2009, serving as both Farage's immediate successor and predecessor, tried to win Cameron over to supporting an In/Out referendum. During the summer of 2009, with Farage's support, Pearson approached Tom Strathclyde, Conservative Leader in the House of Lords, with an offer. If the Tories made a manifesto commitment to hold an In/Out referendum, UKIP would stand down in the coming 2010 election and actively campaign for the Conservatives. While Strathclyde was enthusiastic, Cameron rejected the deal.

Such an agreement could conceivably have been enough to win the Tories an overall majority – but it does not seem likely. At that point, UKIP were not doing well in Westminster elections; their European election votes did not carry over to other votes. For example, UKIP won 2.5 million votes in the 2009 European election on a 35 per cent turnout, but only 900,000 in the 2010 general election on a 65 per cent turnout. It is also far from certain what proportion of UKIP voters would have voted Conservative even if their leaders urged them to do so. Even more of a problem was, whatever UKIP's leaders promised, it seems unlikely that they could have brought all their activists along with them. As a Tory minister put it to us, "Whatever Farage or Pearson would have told the party, the UKIP activists in my patch would still have put up a candidate. They may have had to run under another name – but they would still have run."

In 2010 Cameron was still adamantly opposed to holding an In/Out referendum – but post-Lisbon the only referendum which was now acceptable to his own party's hard-line Eurosceptics was one on Britain's membership of the EU.

Hannan put it thus: "The trigger for me was when Cameron cancelled the commitment to have a referendum on Lisbon, which happened in 2010 because it had been ratified. I resigned from a rather meagre front bench position in the European Parliament. I phoned to let him know I was resigning. I spoke to one of his officials. I said, look this was your last chance to have a referendum on something other than In/Out. There is now going to be a referendum on that. I'm going to make it happen." *€*

Clacton MP Douglas Carswell (left) with Nigel Farage shortly after defecting to UKIP. The change of allegiance kept Europe high on the Prime Minister's agenda.

Stefan Rousseau/PA Archive/Press Association Images

Chapter Two:
An In/Out Referendum: From No to Yes

In his role as a special adviser to then Chancellor Norman Lamont and later to Home Secretary Michael Howard, David Cameron had seen first-hand how the Major government had ripped itself apart over Europe. After becoming Prime Minister in 2010, he was determined to avoid Tory rows over Europe dominating and undermining his own premiership. Cameron's failure to win a majority in the 2010 general election and subsequent decision to enter a coalition with the Liberal Democrats meant that, even if he had wished to make them, any radical moves on Europe would be extremely difficult. The Liberal Democrats in general, and their leader Nick Clegg in particular, regarded support for the European project as perhaps their core leitmotif.

The coalition agreement set out that the new government would introduce legislation which would bind it and any subsequent government (unless, of course, the legislation was repealed) to hold a referendum if a new European treaty, or an amendment to existing treaties, transferred powers from the UK to the EU. This measure – opposed by Labour in the Commons and encountering some difficulties in the House of Lords – became law in July 2011 and was designed as a way for Conservatives and Liberal Democrats to agree to disagree on Europe. The long battles in the UK over whether or not to hold a referendum over this or that EU treaty were now over. It was very unlikely that any future government would repeal this legislation given the inevitable popular backlash against any move to cheat the British public out of a vote. Obviously there could be debate as to whether or not a particular treaty transferred power from the UK to the EU – but any claims by a government denying that such a transfer was taking place could now, and surely would, be challenged in the courts.

In any case, no major new European treaty was on the cards when the referendum lock was agreed on. After so many referendum rejections of treaties by various member countries there was no appetite for one among the EU's heads of government. It did not look as if there would be a UK treaty referendum any time soon.

The one treaty which did then appear on the horizon was a Fiscal Compact Treaty to deal with the escalating economic crisis in the eurozone. It would have been an EU-wide treaty but, dealing as it did with the euro, the UK would not have been directly bound by its provisions. There were, however, grave concerns as to its impact on the City and its possible use to impose new financial encumbrances on the UK, such as the proposed Financial Transactions Tax. Whether this treaty would have been subject to the referendum provisions is debatable. A minor amendment to the EU treaties agreed by European governments in December 2010 to establish a European Stability Mechanism for eurozone states did not require a referendum under the new act as it bound only euro member states and did not transfer further powers from the UK – or so argued the Foreign Secretary, William Hague, in a statement to the Commons on 13 October 2011.

Whether or not a referendum was necessary for the Fiscal Compact Treaty would remain a purely theoretical point. At the European Council meeting of December 2011 Cameron vetoed the proposed treaty as the other heads of government would not agree to safeguards for the City and concrete exemptions for the UK from future financial regulations. This veto greatly boosted Cameron's popularity among even his most hostile Eurosceptic backbenchers – and antagonised his Liberal Democrat coalition partners.

At this stage Cameron was still adamantly opposed to holding an In/Out EU referendum, yet by the summer of 2012 he had changed his mind – by one account, he came round to the idea at a May meeting with his Chief of Staff Ed Llewellyn and Foreign Secretary William Hague held improbably at a pizza restaurant in Chicago's O'Hare airport – and in January 2013 with his so-called Bloomberg speech he went public with his strategy of renegotiation followed by a referendum. What caused this about-turn?

On 24 October 2011 the House of Commons debated a backbench motion, proposed by Conservative MP for Bury North David Nuttall, to call upon the government to bring forward a bill in the next session of parliament (i.e. by early 2013) to hold an In/Out referendum. The government imposed a three-line whip on its MPs to oppose this proposal. The whips did their aggressive best to minimise the size of the rebellion. Yet 81 Tory MPs, alongside 19 Labour rebels and 11 "others" – the "righteous 111" as Daniel Hannan calls them – voted for a referendum. It was the biggest-ever rebellion on Europe against a Conservative government, with almost double the number of MPs who voted against the Major government in the Maastricht rebellions.

MPs generally become more rebellious over time; the longer they are in the job, the less they need the support of the central party. This vote was all the more significant for the fact that 49 of the rebel Tories had first been elected to the Commons only the year before. Cameron was facing a parliamentary party which was much more hostile to European integration than any before. The rebellion made him realise that many in his new cohort of MPs were passionate about their Euroscepticism; for them it was more than a suit of clothes to put on for a constituency selection meeting and then quietly discard in the interests of preferment when safely ensconced on the green benches.

Interestingly, this is an analysis shared by Nigel Farage. He told us: "What was clear was that there was a new intake of Tory MPs in 2010 that were a little bit different to what we'd seen before: a few fewer career politicians, some more people of principle and people prepared to stand against the government. It was clear then that rebellion was in the air. And that it was stronger than the Maastricht rebellions. The Maastricht divisions and rebellions were bitter but in the end, after the end of it all, they said OK chaps and shook hands and said you'd won and we'd lost. It was becoming clear that a new generation of Tories didn't think like that."

There would be further significant rebellions on Europe, not least one led by Mark Reckless – then still a Conservative MP – in October 2012 when 51 backbench MPs voted against Cameron on the EU budget, calling for it to be reduced in real terms. On this occasion the government was defeated as Labour voted with the rebels – although given that the amendment did not bind the government, the loss was only symbolic.

If an In/Out referendum could be won by In – and Cameron believed it could – was it worthwhile antagonising his own party by resisting it? The coalition was creating enough ill-feeling on the Tory backbenches and a referendum pledge would surely make them more compliant. Managing the parliamentary party would be much easier. In any case, without a Tory majority and given the Liberal Democrats' position and the Parliamentary Labour Party's overwhelming pro-Europeanism, such a referendum was an impossibility in the 2010-15 parliament – so any pledge could only be implemented after the 2015 general election, assuming the Conservatives were still in office, a big assumption at that stage.

Cameron also faced increasing pressure from outside parliament. In March 2011 a new campaign for a referendum was launched – the People's Pledge. Its aim was to persuade at least one of the major parties to commit to an In/Out referendum, and to put this into their next general election manifesto. The organisation grew out of the Democracy Movement, the successor to Goldsmith's Referendum Party, and was run by that organisation's Marc-Henri Glendening and Chris Bruni-Lowe, who would later become an important UKIP strategist. Mark Seddon, former editor of the left-wing magazine *Tribune* and one-time member of the Labour Party's National Executive Committee, was recruited to be its director. MPs and other politicians from all parties were brought on board as "supporters" – including a few strong proponents of European integration who still believed in holding a referendum. John Stevens was one such supporter. A Conservative MEP for ten years, he left the party in 1999 to form the Pro-Euro Conservative Party and contest that year's European elections on a federalist ticket.

The innovative tactic that the People's Pledge adopted was to propose holding a rolling programme of constituency referendums to ask voters if they favoured a referendum on EU membership. The question was "Voters should be given a national referendum on whether the UK remains a member of the European Union. Agree or disagree?" The referendums would be organised by and paid for via the People's Pledge but administered and verified by Electoral Reform Services – a body which conducts elections for more than 90 per cent of trade unions and countless voluntary organisations and is seen as the gold standard for running such ballots impartially.

The plan was, if necessary, to hold more than 100 such constituency votes in 2012 and 2013. Votes would be cast by post, telephone or online. Such a campaign would be extremely expensive, but the People's Pledge had a backer who was willing to stump up much of the money: Patrick Barbour, the founder of Barbour Index, a company supplying construction industry data. Barbour had sold his business in 1999 and then devoted much of his energy and wealth not to grand living but to supporting pro-market causes. He not only supported long-established think tanks such as the Institute of Economic Affairs but helped to foster a new generation of organisations. Barbour helped set up and was a major backer of Nick

Herbert's Reform think tank and was an early and substantial supporter of Matthew Elliott's TaxPayers' Alliance. He was now willing to devote his resources to securing an In/Out referendum.

The first referendum to be held was in Thurrock in Essex, later one of the strongest areas for UKIP. Voting closed on 5 April, 2012. Getting a Yes vote was never a problem for the campaign: if you ask the public if they want a referendum on virtually any issue, there will nearly always be a majority in favour of a ballot. The issue was turnout. For these referendums to be taken seriously there would have to be a decent turnout, ideally on a par with that for local elections. In Thurrock the turnout was just over 30 per cent of the electorate, of whom nearly 90 per cent agreed with the proposition. The turnout was three percentage points higher than for that year's local elections in Thurrock. There were two subsequent referendums, in August 2012 in Cheadle and Hazel Grove, neighbouring constituencies in suburban Greater Manchester. The turnouts, at around 35 per cent, were higher than in Thurrock and the results were very similar.

Planned further referendums were cancelled. There were to be ten constituencies in the next batch but it was gradually becoming clear that Cameron would agree to an In/Out referendum. Hannan, who was involved in launching the People's Pledge, says: "It is the most successful pressure group I have ever known – founded in 2011 and by January 2013 it had succeeded. When we launched, everyone said, forget it. Cameron said, forget it. When I told Ed Llewellyn [Cameron's chief of staff] what I was doing he said, 'ha ha ha, good luck with that'."

How important the People's Pledge was in changing Cameron's mind is debatable. It was not the first time a privately-funded referendum had taken place in the UK. In 2000 the same tactic was used for a rather different purpose in Scotland. The devolved Scottish government was in the process of repealing what was popularly known as Clause 28, a measure passed by the Thatcher government in 1988 which stated that a local authority could no longer "intentionally promote homosexuality" or "promote the teaching in any maintained school of the acceptability of homosexuality as a pretended family relationship". Whether this had ever occurred is doubtful. Nevertheless, Brian Souter, the founder of the bus operator Stagecoach, was greatly upset by its repeal and spent more than £1 million to organise a postal referendum of all Scottish voters to ask them if they supported its repeal. He too hoped that Electoral Reform Services would conduct the poll but in this instance it refused, stating that it would not be a legitimate democratic exercise as the public would not know what the alternative to the clause was. The poll went ahead anyway, and the results were remarkably similar to those for the People's Pledge referendums. There was a turnout of just over 30 per cent and nearly 87 per cent of those who voted supported retaining the clause. Yet the Scottish vote made little difference: the clause was repealed. (The failure of his initiative did not diminish Souter's enthusiasm for referendums: in 2014 he donated £1.4 million to the SNP's campaign for independence in the Scottish referendum. He was the second-largest donor to the cause of Scottish independence, after Colin and Christine Weir, an Ayrshire couple who won £161 million on the Euromillions lottery in 2011.)

The People's Pledge did put pressure on Cameron. But he surely would not have changed his mind if it were not for the strong parliamentary support for a referendum, which was admittedly reinforced when backbenchers saw the outcomes of the local referendums – and the growing threat from UKIP.

In 2011 Stuart Wheeler, who had made his fortune by setting up IG Index, the UK's first spread betting firm, had become UKIP's Treasurer. When he first came onto the political scene with his munificent donation to the Tories in 2001, Wheeler was not particularly interested in Europe as a political issue; he simply wanted a Conservative government elected again after the party's 1997 drubbing. It was conversations with Rodney Leach that kindled Wheeler's passion for Euroscepticism, a path which eventually led him to UKIP.

Wheeler still had strong Tory contacts and he used these to the full to increase pressure on Cameron. On becoming actively involved in UKIP in 2011, Wheeler invited ten Tory MPs to lunch; eight accepted and were happy to explore the possibility of defecting. The fact that these lunches had occurred was made known to the press and contributed to the febrile atmosphere in the Conservative Party. Farage says of the time: "The newspapers were awash with who Stuart Wheeler had wined and dined, who I'd met, who I was talking to or not talking to. It was quite a widespread fear that half a dozen-plus [Tory MPs] would come over." The fear of defections – especially in light of backbench unhappiness about the coalition – certainly contributed to Cameron's referendum pledge.

UKIP had historically only performed well in European elections but during 2011 the party began to make something of a showing in general election opinion polls; their support went up from two or three per cent to seven or eight per cent. During 2012 UKIP's increase in support grew dramatically, with it polling ahead of the Liberal Democrats for the first time in some general election surveys and frequently getting into double figures. At the time, the narrative was still that UKIP was mainly a threat to the Tories and that the vast majority of these votes were coming from naturally Conservative supporters. With hindsight, it is clear that this was not the case and that the party was at least as much a threat to Labour. The fear of defections and the rise of UKIP in the polls is why Wheeler still believes with certainty – regardless of the fact that he was very much not a supporter of Farage's strategy in the immediate run-up to and during the referendum campaign, serving for a time on the board of the rival Vote Leave referendum campaign and donating at least £615,000 to it – that if it were not for Farage we would not have had a referendum.

Cameron's much-trailed Bloomberg speech – even though it set out how the EU needed to be reformed, in the broadest terms, and made clear the plan to renegotiate and then hold a referendum – was probably the most Europhile speech he had made up to that point in his career. It left open the possibility that he would support Britain leaving the EU if it could not be reformed, but any fair commentator listening to it would have been very surprised if the Prime Minister did anything other than lead the Remain side in the event of a referendum. Cameron emphasised his belief that it was vital for Britain to remain a member of the European Single Market and that the Norwegian and Swiss models of being a member of the Single Market but not of the EU would create all but insurmountable difficulties for the UK. The speech made clear that certain protections were needed for non-euro members within the European Union and also that Britain should be excluded from ever closer union even though other members might wish to pursue it. But its whole tenor was about the need to reform the EU as a whole, not to obtain a special status for the UK.

Cameron was aware that little could be achieved in terms of a referendum before the next general election in 2015; the Liberal Democrats would not countenance any moves towards holding a referendum or allow preparatory referendum legislation to go forward as a government bill. There was no mention of a referendum bill in the 2013

Queen's Speech outlining the government's programme for the coming session of parliament, and 130 MPs, including 114 Tory backbenchers, voted for a motion expressing their "regret" at this.

In every parliamentary session a number of backbench MPs can introduce their own bills with the guarantee of being given a certain amount of the House's time. At the start of the session there is a ballot – a random selection chosen by lot – that decides which backbenchers have first dibs at introducing a Private Member's Bill. Only those who come in the top six or seven have any chance of their favoured proposal becoming law.

James Wharton, the MP for Stockton South and at 29 then the youngest Tory in the Commons, came top of the ballot for the 2013-14 session of parliament and announced that he would – along the lines of what was now Cameron's policy – introduce a bill to legislate for an In/Out referendum by the end of 2017. Any Tory Eurosceptic who had topped the ballot would have done the same. The Conservative leadership reluctantly agreed to support the bill, whipping their MPs in its favour, knowing full well that it would be unlikely to make it into law. The bill passed its Second Reading by 304 votes to nil – it was Labour and Lib Dem policy to abstain. After delaying tactics by its opponents the Wharton bill passed all its Commons stages but was then stopped in the House of Lords when, in January 2014, hostile peers voted not to provide any further time for debate. In the 2014-15 session of parliament Bob Neill, the MP for Bromley and Chislehurst, coming third, was the top Tory in the Private Member's Bill ballot. He introduced an identical bill to Wharton's but while it was again passed at Second Reading it failed to make further progress in the Commons. (During the referendum campaign, while Wharton campaigned strongly for Leave, Neill was a supporter of Remain, largely on the grounds that Brexit would be bad for Gibraltar.)

If the Tories were to win the 2015 general election it was by now clear that there would be an In/Out referendum. Any attempt by Cameron or any other Tory Prime Minister to renege on what would certainly be a central manifesto commitment would have ripped the Conservative Party apart and it is difficult to see how such a leader could have survived the backlash from his or her MPs.

The issue then was whether the Tories would win a majority. Very few commentators – and even fewer opinion polls – suggested that this was possible. The scenario which was seen as more likely – that there would be a renewed Conservative/Liberal Democrat coalition albeit with the Lib Dems considerably weakened – would in all likelihood also have led to an In/Out referendum. The Lib Dems would have been in a weak position to resist, and dropping the referendum pledge would have been much too high a price for many Conservative MPs. It seems unlikely that Cameron could have got any coalition deal to stick, especially since he had agreed to consult his MPs before any second coalition was entered into, without keeping to his referendum pledge. It was also clear that Nick Clegg was beginning to believe that an In/Out referendum at some stage in the future was becoming inevitable. The only thing which would now stop there being a referendum was if the general election produced a Labour, or Labour-led, government.

In 2014 Labour leader Ed Miliband pledged that if further powers were transferred to the EU a Labour government would hold an In/Out referendum, rather than a referendum on the treaty changes. Miliband made clear, however, that he thought such a transfer of powers was unlikely to happen soon, and expected that there would be no referendum while he was Prime Minister. Lord Owen, who while not rejoining Labour had made donations of £18,000 to the party under Miliband's leadership, attempted to convince Miliband to make a commitment to holding an In/Out referendum during the lifetime of the 2015 parliament. (Owen did not favour a pledge to hold a referendum by 2017 as he thought that it should happen after the French and German elections of that year, in the hope that Britain could negotiate a better deal at that stage.) Miliband rejected this idea, arguing that a referendum commitment would destroy his premiership and ensure that Labour would not win a second term. If the Tories had lost the 2015 election, Miliband believed they would elect a pro-Brexit leader, and a referendum in 2018 with a united Tory party calling for a Leave vote would be impossible to win for the Remain side. Ironically, if Miliband had agreed to an In/Out referendum, polling indicates that Labour would have had a better chance of winning the 2015 general election – 19 per cent of voters would have been more likely to vote Labour and only 8 per cent would have been less likely.

Where Cameron's Bloomberg speech failed spectacularly was in seeing off UKIP. In the local elections of May 2013 – the first elections other than Europeans in which the party did seriously well – UKIP gained 22 per cent of the vote, just three percentage points behind the Tories. During that summer UKIP hit 20 per cent and higher in various general election opinion polls. As Farage put it, "The irony was that far from shoot the UKIP fox, all the Bloomberg speech did was feed it."

In May 2014 the European elections were to be held. This would give UKIP a huge opportunity in a set of elections where they had a history of doing well and in the run-up to which they would, based on their second-place showing in the previous elections in 2009, get a great deal of TV airtime because of broadcasting impartiality rules. In an attempt to stymie UKIP's advance Clegg – remembering how well he had done in the 2010 general election debates – challenged Farage to TV debates on Europe. This move was disastrous for the pro-Europeans and further boosted UKIP. Although many pundits at first thought Clegg had the better of the argument, the public saw Farage as the clear winner of both contests in March and April 2014; one poll showed that Farage had won the second debate by 68 to 27 per cent.

During the European election campaign UKIP was relentlessly attacked by the other parties and in much of the press. Day after day another UKIP councillor or candidate was discovered to have come out with this or that nutty pronouncement. Nevertheless, UKIP topped the poll – the first time a party other than Conservative or Labour had won a national election since 1910 or, arguably, 1906 – with nearly 27 per cent of the vote and 24 out of 73 seats. The Liberal Democrats – running as "the party of In" – were reduced to one seat, losing ten. It seemed that all the mud thrown at UKIP had little effect, although two Tory MPs we have spoken to – one a reluctant Remainer, the other a strong Leaver – take a different view. They both think that the campaign against UKIP was highly effective. From their experience on the doorstep they believe that UKIP could easily have gained a third or more in this low-turnout election – it was 35 per cent – if it were not for the campaign against it.

The surge in UKIP support created great tensions on the Leave side, as many of its backers came to believe that there was an inverse relationship between support for UKIP and support for leaving the EU. Hannan put it to us thus: "From the beginning of the euro crisis, in 2008, there were big majorities for leaving the EU across the UK, until UKIP began its rise to prominence, which was much more recent than we now think. UKIP was a tiny fringe party that nobody could name until 2013, when Nigel started appearing on Question Time every other week and it became a huge issue. As he became more prominent, it is what Sunder Katwala [former general secretary of the Fabian Society, the Labour think tank, and now director of British Future, a think tank dealing with immigration and integration issues] kept calling the Farage paradox: the better UKIP did the further support for leaving the EU fell. It was an almost exact correlation and the reason for that, I'm pretty sure, is that the case for leaving the EU was being put in essentially negative terms. It was pessimistic and nostalgic rather than optimistic and forward-looking. Between 2013 and the beginning of this campaign we fell further and further behind. And break it down. Among whom did we fall further and further behind? Which were the demographic groups among whom we started losing support most swiftly? It was very clear it was women, ethnic minorities, and, above all, young people. Now, I cannot believe that is because the EU was doing anything right at that time. It was because of the way Euroscepticism was being presented as an essentially angry and negative project."

Hannan is clearly overstating his case for effect when he argues that UKIP was a tiny fringe party that nobody could name until 2013. After all, they had beaten the Lib Dems in the 2004 European elections, and the Lib Dems and Labour in the 2009 elections. The broader point, though, that UKIP's rise, especially in terms of general election support, was later than many now remember, is absolutely correct. It is also undeniable that support for leaving the EU fell during that period.

What is curious is that Hannan's two closest political allies – Douglas Carswell, Conservative MP for Clacton, and Mark Reckless, Conservative MP for Rochester and Strood – would now play a major role in further boosting UKIP. On 28 August 2014 Carswell defected to UKIP and announced that he would resign his seat to fight a by-election under his new political colours. A month later, on 27 September, during the Clacton by-election campaign, Reckless came to the UKIP party conference and announced that he too would be defecting, triggering another by-election. Reckless had considered defecting earlier and come close to doing so the previous autumn.

Both MPs retained their seats. In the case of Carswell this was never in doubt as Clacton is by some demographic measures the most UKIP-friendly seat in the country. In October he won with nearly 60 per cent of the vote with the biggest swing ever seen in a UK by-election. In its immediate aftermath, polls put UKIP general election support at up to 25 per cent. In November Reckless had a much tougher fight on his hands but prevailed. He would be less fortunate six months later.

The European elections and the by-elections raised expectations among UKIP members enormously. Many believed that they would win dozens of seats in the 2015 general election. They were to be sorely disappointed: while gaining nearly 13 per cent of the vote and 3.8 million votes they ended up with only one seat, Clacton.

What motivated Carswell's defection? A major part of it was to increase pressure on Cameron, but he also had another motive. Carswell believed that by defecting to UKIP he could "detoxify" the party and this could help overcome the Farage paradox. If UKIP were detoxified, or so his thinking went, it would be easier for Leave to win the referendum. This is certainly the explanation that has been put to us for Carswell's defection by someone who is very well placed to know the Clacton MP's motives. The speech Carswell gave on defecting to UKIP – with its optimism about the future, warnings against looking back to a mythical past, and emphasis on being happy with the country as it now is – supports that thesis. The concerns of Carswell and Hannan about the supposed toxicity of Farage and UKIP prefigured later battles over the Leave side's referendum strategy. *C*

Matthew Elliott, the low-tax campaigner, ran Business for Britain and, later, Vote Leave.

Picture by: Dominic Lipinski/PA Wire/Press Association Images

Chapter Three:
Building the Brexit Coalition

Eurosceptics didn't need David Cameron's Bloomberg speech to know that a referendum on Britain's membership of the European Union was on its way. The combined pressure exerted from within the Parliamentary Conservative Party and from without – from UKIP, the press, campaign groups such as the People's Pledge and others – had, for many, simply become too great for Cameron not to respond.

Cameron had indeed made his mind up on offering a referendum long before his speech at Bloomberg's London offices early on 23 January 2013. His impromptu Chicago pizza summit with Hague and Llewellyn had taken place some nine months earlier, on 21 May 2012. In June 2012, John Baron MP delivered a letter to Cameron signed by 100 MPs calling for legislation on a referendum before the general election and arguing that "whatever one's views on the EU" a statutory commitment to a referendum "would address the very real lack of public trust when people hear politicians making promises". Cameron's response hinted at a referendum promise: "I don't think it is in Britain's interests to leave the EU but what I do think is it is increasingly becoming the time for a new settlement between Britain and Europe, and I think that new settlement will require fresh consent."

By 2012, Daniel Hannan was sufficiently convinced that a referendum was on its way to move his attention from the work of securing a vote on EU membership to the question of how to win that contest. For the Conservative MEP this was the endgame of a lifelong battle. Late in 1990, between Margaret Thatcher leaving Downing Street (22 November) and John Major initialing a draft of the Maastricht Treaty (6 December), Hannan met two fellow Oxford undergraduates, one of whom was Mark Reckless, in the Queen's Cafe on Oxford High Street. There they founded the Oxford Campaign for an Independent Britain, a fogeyish organisation that made a name for itself by disrupting speeches at Conservative party conferences and organising flag-waving trips to the Last Night of the Proms. Hannan recounted to us a trip to London by the foreign minister of Latvia, recently freed from its Soviet rule. "He said, 'Latvia is now more independent than the United Kingdom,' which of course it was. And that was the moment I decided that this was the chief cause in British politics and that I was going to devote my life to getting us out." In 1999, he was elected as an MEP.

A quarter of a century after that meeting in an Oxford coffee shop, the British people were – if the Conservative Party could only clear the hurdle of the general election – going to be given the opportunity to declare that independence. Hannan knew exactly who he wanted to run the campaign.

Matthew Elliott is a career campaigner and lobbyist for conservative causes. Many Brexiteers relish their (often phoney) outsider status. They love to play up their detachment from the bubble, feigning ignorance of how members of the political establishment do business. Not Elliott, who trades off insider know-how. Emollient, polite and softly-spoken, Elliott earned a reputation as an effective operator at the TaxPayers' Alliance, a low-tax pressure group he founded with Andrew Allum in 2004. It took as its inspiration the high jinks of American libertarian campaigner Grover Norquist, who founded and still runs Americans for Tax Reform. By disseminating outlandish tales of wasteful government expenditure, working within Westminster and with the backing of wealthy Tory donors while posing as a "grassroots" movement, and concentrating on clearly-defined hard-to-disagree-with campaigns on tax and spending issues, the TPA and its bright young chief executive quickly grew in influence. In 2009 Elliott applied his campaigning nous to Big Brother Watch, which he co-founded with Richard Smith to fight the surveillance state. He also had a Eurosceptic pedigree. His first job was for one of the Brexit movement's founding fathers, working as a press officer for Bill Cash's European Foundation.

Hannan approached Elliott at what he describes as a "sound" gathering in the garden of Open Europe founder Rodney Leach's Norfolk home in the summer of 2012, where the guests included conservative philosopher Roger Scruton. He sounded Elliott out. "Are you prepared to do this?" he asked, "because if you are, then we can set about raising money for it and putting the infrastructure in place." Elliott's mind was made up: he too wanted to get Britain out of the EU.

Elliott's eligibility for running the Leave campaign came not from the TaxPayers' Alliance or Big Brother Watch, but from the success of the No to AV campaign he had led the previous year. The decisive result Elliott and his team delivered in that 2011 referendum – a winning margin of 67.9

per cent to 32.1 per cent, or a gap of nearly seven million votes on a turnout of 45 per cent and clear evidence that public opinion swung emphatically in their direction during the campaign – buried the issue of electoral reform for the foreseeable future.

Elliott had caught Hannan's eye not simply because of the "awesome" No to AV victory, but because of the characteristics he had demonstrated during the campaign. Elliott had shown great imperturbability in the face of criticism from his own side, something Hannan knew would be valuable in a European referendum, whenever that happened. "You can absorb almost unlimited ordnance from the enemy," said Hannan, "but [Elliott] had been criticised very heavily by our own side and that is the toughest thing in politics." Under Elliott's leadership, the No to AV campaign had pursued an eccentric line of argument against a new voting system that centred on cost. One No to AV poster showed a crying new-born baby in a doctor's hands alongside the words "She needs a maternity unit NOT an alternative voting system. Say NO to spending £250 million on AV. Our country can't afford it." Another poster argued that a soldier needed a bulletproof vest, not a new voting system. To focus on what is a trivial sum in relation to overall government spending rather than stand by the merits of first past the post brought opprobrium even from sympathetic newspapers. Cost, however, was the line of attack that most resonated in focus groups. "It was the worst argument going," said Hannan, who saw obvious flaws in it. "But Matthew stuck to his numbers and the messages that he knew were going to work rather than to the intuitive views of various leader writers."

No to AV's success had not only sent Elliott to the top of the list of candidates to run the Leave campaign, it also influenced how he and his team planned to pull off the more formidable feat of securing a Leave vote in an EU referendum. Subsequently, Elliott has described No to AV as "a test run for a possible EU referendum". But the two polls were very different challenges. In 2011, Elliott and his team had much of the political establishment on their side and their sell was comparatively easy: don't side with Nick Clegg and his complicated voting machines, stick with a tried and tested way of delivering strong government. Persuading Britain to vote to leave the EU would, by contrast, mean arguing against the status quo, practically every major multinational corporation, almost every foreign leader and the majority of the political establishment. If they pulled it off they would have convinced the country to commit the single most revolutionary democratic act since the extension of the franchise.

Compared to a general election, a referendum is a straightforward contest. There are no marginal seats, just two boxes on the ballot paper, two sides to choose between. The victory line is simple: half of the votes plus one. Tactics that bring out the core vote in one marginal seat and squeeze voters in another are redundant. A conservative approach with limited appeal beyond the hard core committed to leaving the EU no matter what was doomed to fail. Polling published in *How Deeply Does Britain's Euroscepticism Run?*, a January 2016 British Social Attitudes study by Professor John Curtice, indicated that while 65 per cent of British voters were sceptical about the EU and wanted it to have less power, just 30 per cent supported withdrawal.

As early as 2012, it was clear that, given the electorate's lack of enthusiasm for the European project, the case made by Remain campaigners would be pragmatic. Brexiteers understood that for most people, it wasn't as straightforward as In/Out – Euroscepticism was a spectrum. Victory lay in winning round Eurosceptic but undecided voters.

Curtice's survey found that 40 per cent thought leaving the EU would have a negative impact on the economy, while 24 per cent thought the effect would be positive. The poll's most instructive finding was that just 6 per cent of voters who thought Brexit would be economically damaging would vote Leave. In other words neither campaign could afford to ignore the economics of Brexit.

For Leave campaigners, the experience of the AV referendum bore this out. As well as focusing on cost early on, the Elliott-led No side also fought their opponents on which electoral system was fairer. Given that the opposing campaign called itself "Yes! To Fairer Votes", one can assume they thought fairness was comfortable territory. They were expecting what one campaigner describes as a "bulldog and Union Jack" defence of British parliamentary democracy. Instead, No to AV rebutted their opponents head-on, claiming it was their system that was fairer. Lord Reid, who led Labour No to AV, summed up this view when he claimed that the campaign was about "defending the right of one person, one vote" and "a system that gives exactly the same voting rights to every single person, irrespective of background or station in life".

As with AV, so too with Europe. Elliott and his team planned an all-out attack on the economic case for Remain: "We thought we could at least fight Project Fear to a standstill, by looking at their main arguments and trying to knock them down one by one," said one campaigner. But with the Brexit campaign, Elliott would claim to reach new heights of counter-intuitive campaigning. Not only would they lead off with what was widely perceived as the Leave camp's weakest argument, to begin with, they wouldn't even make clear which side they took on EU membership.

Less than a month after Cameron's Bloomberg speech, an organisation putting forward Eurosceptic economic arguments without – for now – being explicitly pro-withdrawal was founded. Business for Britain was founded with Matthew Elliott, William Norton (who had been the referendum agent for No to AV) and Daniel Hodson (a Eurosceptic financier) as directors. It operated out of the same Westminster address as the TaxPayers' Alliance.

In March, James Forsyth wrote in his *Mail on Sunday* column that "David Cameron's push to change Britain's EU membership terms will soon receive a boost when a group called Business for Britain is launched. It is the brainchild of Matthew Elliott . . . and is modelled on Business for Sterling, which played a crucial role in keeping the country out of the euro. The group will represent the mainstream against extremes of the European debate and has already attracted considerable support, including from one Labour donor." A *Sun* headline from April read: "PM's EU bid gets business backing". The press, then, had bought Elliott's conceit of agnosticism on EU membership.

Elliott himself announced the arrival of his organisation with an article in the *Sunday Times* on 21 April:

> Faced with this unhappy situation the kneejerk reaction of many has been to say that the time has come to ditch the EU and race off into the great unknown. With the constant drip of stories about Brussels waste, barmy regulations and powers being transferred to the EU against our wishes, it's understandable that many now feel leaving the EU would be the best option. But the sensible approach, articulated by the Prime Minister in his Bloomberg speech in January, is to sit down with our European neighbours and see if we can work out a deal that we can all be happy with.

Not, on the surface, the words of a man committed to leaving the European

Union, as he had told Hannan he was the previous summer. Elliott's disingenuous balancing act in which he argued for reforming the EU to avoid a surge in support for leaving positioned Business for Britain as a campaign that "the vast majority – who don't want 'out' but are fed up with the current 'in'– can support". Disingenuousness was commonplace in the Europe debate. Business for Britain's stance mirrored that of the Prime Minister, who, less convincingly, refused to rule out advocating a Leave vote if he did not get the reforms he wanted.

If Business for Britain's broad goal was to "fight Project Fear at least to a standstill", one of its more specific objectives was to place in the public consciousness a distinction between the views of the CBI (a consistently pro-integration business lobby group long loathed by Eurosceptics) and big business, and the broader business community. They commissioned a poll by YouGov which found that 46 per cent of British business leaders said the costs of complying with the single market outweighed the benefits of being in the EU, with 36 per cent taking the opposite view.

Business for Britain's lack of clarity on the all-important EU membership question fooled not only the press, but also the business leaders that signed up to their campaign. While the organisation's board was dominated by full-blooded Eurosceptics, with Alan Halsall and John Mills as co-chairmen, it signed up a far broader group of supporters. In fact, the spectrum of scepticism it embraced was so wide that it included Tory peer and former M&S chairman Stuart Rose, who would go on to (briefly and ingloriously) lead the Remain campaign. Just a few months after its launch, Business for Britain boasted more than 500 business people supporting its economic case for renegotiation. The organisation quickly established itself as a Eurosceptic but centrist voice that added to the chorus of criticism of the EU which, throughout 2014 – a year in which UKIP won the European elections and two parliamentary by-elections – kept EU reform and the promise of a referendum high on the agenda.

Few Leavers could find fault with a high-profile organisation making the economic case against the European Union. However, the idea that Business for Britain would – without challenge – morph into the official Leave campaign, as Elliott and Hannan hoped, irked some. In particular, UKIP politicians and supporters felt that, given it was their hard work and the popular appeal of Nigel Farage that had forced Cameron to promise a referendum in the first place, the generals of the self-styled People's Army deserved a leading role in the fight to take the UK out of the EU. Further, they argued that they had experience of mobilising mass support behind an anti-EU stance.

Euroscepticism has always been a broad church. Just as the affiliations of the EU's critics stretch across the political spectrum and differences between Brexiteers' reasons for wanting the UK to leave the EU were diverse to the point of direct contradiction, Leave campaigners differed on the best tactics for a referendum campaign. To the UKIP wing, an Elliott-led operation would be fought from within "the bubble", whereas only an anti-politics, anti-Westminster, anti-elite campaign could possibly galvanise enough support to win.

Despite these differences, there was a strong incentive for those who happened to agree that the UK should leave the EU to work together: the designation of an official Leave campaign. Under the Political Parties, Election and Referendum Act 2000, the Electoral Commission designates an organisation as the lead campaigner for each side of a referendum. Designation comes with several crucial perks: a spending limit of £7 million (as opposed to £700,000 for non-designated organisations or individuals), a free mailshot to voters (worth several million pounds), campaign broadcast time and £600,000 of government money. In the event of more than one organisation applying for designation, the Electoral Commission must choose between them by considering how the candidate's objectives fit with the referendum outcome it supports; the breadth and level of support for the organisation; how the organisation plans to represent other groups on their side of the referendum; and its capacity to deliver the campaign.

Few could have thought the Electoral Commission would have to decide between different Brexit groups; given the uphill struggle ahead of them, Leavers were adamant they could not afford to waste time fighting one another. The obstacles that stood between hard-line Eurosceptics and a Leave victory were legion: securing a majority for the Conservatives, making sure the promise of a referendum was delivered, levelling the campaign playing field, and then taking on and defeating the political establishment, received economic wisdom and the machinery of government.

***

From his first foray into national politics, Arron Banks did not hide his hot-headedness. On the morning of David Cameron's 2014 party conference speech, UKIP announced that a Conservative donor would be defecting to the party. That donor was Banks, whose donations to the Conservatives had been modest and who William Hague told the BBC he had "never heard of". Banks had planned to give UKIP £100,000 but Hague's dismissive riposte annoyed him so much that he upped his contribution to £1 million. "Now he knows who I am," Banks told the press. This would not be the last instance of bolshie grandstanding from the Bristol-based businessman.

Banks's involvement in UKIP continued through the general election campaign, during which he devoted both time and money to the party's ultimately unsuccessful attempt to break through at the parliamentary level. Yet for committed Leavers like Banks, there was considerable consolation in the fact that the Conservatives' unexpected majority meant an imminent referendum on EU membership was now all but certain.

Shortly after the result, Banks met Richard Tice, another businessman who was keen not to squander the chance to leave the EU. Tice had been involved in the campaign to keep the pound and, though not a member of UKIP, had given the party money in the past. He and Banks were frustrated with what they saw as inaction from the Westminster Leave camp and concerned that the Remainers were stealing a march on them.

"We both had a clear view just after the election," Tice told us, "that nothing was happening on the Leave side." Tice and Banks were adamant that the sooner a campaign group was up and running, the better. As they saw it, Cameron was basking in the glory of his electoral success, his poll numbers were soaring and the arguments for leaving the EU were "getting killed" in the media. In particular, Banks and Tice were frustrated by Business for Britain's continued ambivalence on the actual referendum question. Convinced there needed to be an explicit Out campaign up and running and able to rebut the Remain arguments before they took hold, the two businessmen saw no reason to leave it to the politicians. Instead, they decided to set up a campaign of their own. They appointed an advertising agency and creative team who recommended they call the group The Know. (At the time the referendum question was set to be "Should the United Kingdom remain a member of the Europen Union?" with a Yes or No option; their slogan was to be "If you're in the know, you'll vote no.")

By late May Banks and Elliott were in touch with each other, beginning attempts to coordinate the Leave side. "It might be a good idea to meet up shortly," wrote Banks, in one of many in a series of previously unseen emails between senior Leave campaigners. "We are working on a campaign for No in the referendum that will be non-political – which has major money behind it – we intend to launch in two months with a bang. The idea will be to run it like the British Olympic bid – high octane with sports business and entertainment people . . . "

While Banks and Tice were the fastest out the blocks after the election, applying what Tice described as their "no bullshit, businesslike approach", their suspicion that nothing meaningful was happening in Westminster was not quite right. Across the river, in a kitchen in Kennington, a group of MPs who had grown to trust one another over years of ignoring party whips and opposing transfers of money, power and just about anything else from the UK to Brussels gathered. They had expected to be discussing an Owen Paterson leadership bid in the wake of a Conservative election defeat. (He would have led the Eurosceptic charge had Cameron resigned.) Instead, sitting at Bernard Jenkin's kitchen table, they found themselves discussing how to approach an EU referendum. Jenkin pinpoints this moment as when he decided he would be for Leave. "It was obvious that David Cameron was not serious about renegotiation," he told us, though this seems an implausibly late conversion for such a die-hard Eurosceptic. Also present were Matthew Elliott and a new face to many in the Leave camp, someone who would go on to position himself in an ever more central role in the campaign: Dominic Cummings.

Blunt, rude, impatient, difficult, arrogant. These are all words that have been used to describe the Conservative campaigner to us. Cummings's reputation for divisiveness was so great that the Prime Minister's spokesman Andy Coulson, with the backing of his boss, vetoed his entry into government in 2010. And yet despite these unhelpful eccentricities, Cummings has earned a reputation for political genius. One Leave politician described him as having "a brain the size of the planet". As a special adviser to Michael Gove at the Department for Education, Cummings's ruthlessness helped his boss to run the most pro-active and radically reforming ministry in Cameron's government. Unsurprisingly, however, many found him difficult to work with. A meeting of the Department for Education's ministers, as recounted by David Laws in his memoir *Coalition*, gives a flavour of Cummings's directness:

> After [Gove] has finished speaking, he asked who else wanted to comment.
>
> From the far end of the table a scruffy, unshaven figure put up his hand to speak – Dom Cummings.
>
> "When I first came to this department in 2011, I said we should sack half of the staff. I was told it would be impossible and the department would collapse. Well, we have done it, and who actually noticed? Now I think we need to go even further. We should sack all the incompetent people. There are far too many white men in their middle fifties in this department who are no good."
>
> At this moment, a lot of white, mid-fifties men around the table looked down at their papers. But Mr Cummings was not finished.
>
> "They should be sacked and replaced by young women in their twenties and thirties. Oh, and one last thing. We need to stop stupid initiatives from No. 10 and from Clegg."

Afterwards, Cummings told Laws, "If people in the Deputy Prime Minister's office think I've 'gone rogue', they ain't seen nothing yet." Clegg's memoir, *Politics: Between the Extremes*, does not mention Cummings by name but nevertheless clearly shows that the antipathy was mutual. A person who could only be Cummings is described as "unhinged".

Cummings's presence in the Leave camp – he was there at the invitation of Bernard Jenkin, who had worked with him on the North East Says No regional government referendum campaign in 2004 – raised eyebrows not simply because of the reputation for being difficult that preceded him. Throughout 2015 Cummings kept a blog, on which he published his thoughts on the forthcoming referendum. One post, published in late June, was on "Exit plans and a second referendum". In it he wrote: "One can see why NO might argue for a second vote. It enables NO to make a NO vote seem much less risky. 'If you vote YES, you won't get another vote for another 40 years – if ever. You should vote No to Cameron's rubbish deal. If you vote NO, you will force a new Government to negotiate a new deal and give you a new vote. *A NO vote is much safer than a YES vote.*' Further, as a matter of democratic accountability, given the enormous importance of so many issues that would be decided in an Article 50 renegotiation – a far, far bigger deal than a normal election – it seems right to give people a vote on it." He went on: "Expanding the debate to consider a second negotiation and a second referendum offers potential disadvantages . . . I have not reached any conclusion. These are the sort of things that need to be discussed BEFORE a NO campaign launches officially." By airing different theories on how best to fight the campaign and including the idea of a second referendum, Cummings was pulling at one of the greatest tensions between Leave campaigners: suspicions that the commitment to leaving the EU was less than sincere for some of them. In particular, UKIP campaigners, including Banks, were wary of Tories using an EU referendum to fight party leadership battles.

On 18 June, seven MPs released a statement announcing the formation of an Exploratory Committee for an EU referendum. The group was made up of three Conservatives (Steve Baker, Bernard Jenkin and Owen Paterson), three from Labour (Kate Hoey, Kelvin Hopkins and Graham Stringer) and Douglas Carswell, UKIP's sole MP. The statement said "there is no sign of any proposals [...] to end the supremacy of EU law over UK law" and that the MPs would be setting up an Exploratory Committee (ExCom) to plan a Leave campaign:

> In order to match the Bloomberg commitment, that "it is national parliaments, which are, and will remain, the true source of real democratic legitimacy and accountability in the EU", the UK's national parliament must be able to decide such vital matters as the level of UK taxpayer contributions to the EU budget, what regulations should apply to UK business, how to control immigration from the EU, and the UK's trade relations with non-EU countries.
>
> Without this, we believe that the best interests of the UK, Europe, the wider world, and the cause of peaceful international cooperation, would be advanced by the UK leaving the EU and pursuing a different relationship with our EU partners. We still hope, and urge, the government will listen to, and understand, these concerns.
>
> The referendum will be a historic turning point. Both sides will require the creation of substantial organisations to provide voters with a real choice. There are therefore many issues that need urgent attention, including . . . how an OUT campaign might best be formed and run to inform the public about the issues.
>
> We are therefore forming a cross-party group to consider these

questions. This is not the 'OUT' campaign, but we are seeking urgently to provide resources for crucial thinking and to promote cooperation amongst those who might contribute to an OUT campaign.

To keep up appearances, Matthew Elliott commented on the launch in his capacity as Chief Executive of Business for Britain, with *The Times* quoting him welcoming the group: "It's absolutely right there is a professional, cross-party campaign for 'Out'. If Britain can't secure the changes we need then it's vital the case to leave an unreformed EU is made loudly and clearly." This statement put the embryonic Parliamentary Leave movement out in the open. *The Times* also reported that Dominic Cummings was "overseeing" the committee, something denied on his blog. He clarified: "I've gone to lots of meeting, talked to people about possible lessons from other things I've done like the euro and North East referendum campaigns (and mistakes we made), how a professional NO campaign should be structured, etc . . . I go to [ExCom] meetings, listen and give advice . . . I will not be 'running the NO campaign'. I am helping people get something started . . . Soon I will return to my studies."

Cummings's insistence that his role was limited is certainly at odds with the emails sent between senior Leave campaigners at the time. Elliott and Cummings presented themselves as a team. At one stage Elliott even referred to himself and Cummings as a "package deal".

By late June, attempts to bring the Brexit family together were in full swing. Banks and Tice invited senior Leavers including Baker, Jenkin, Paterson, Carswell, Cummings, Elliott, Mills, Hannan and Ruth Lea, a leading Leave economist, to a meeting at the Corinthia Hotel, near Trafalgar Square, "to put forward our thinking and approach as well as to present the work in progress of the creative agency who we have had working hard on the brief for some three weeks now". One participant said the group left "unimpressed" with their allies' efforts.

Cummings had his own ideas about what a Leave campaign should look like. Writing on his blog in early July, he complained that building a NO campaign "should have started years ago". He argued against the idea of waiting until Cameron's renegotiation was over – something Elliott had appeared to favour. After quoting one of his heroes, Otto Von Bismarck – "Better to be a hammer than an anvil . . . If revolution there is to be, better to undertake it than undergo it" – he posted a series of videos the No campaign should emulate. They were: Sergei Eisenstein's silent film *October: Ten Days That Shook The World*, a work of communist propaganda; LBJ's provocative "Daisy" attack ad from the 1964 US Presidential election, which warned that a vote for his opponent, Barry Goldwater, risked nuclear holocaust; and Apple's iconic "1984" advertisement for the Macintosh which promised to make consumers "see why 1984 won't be like *1984*". "Do you want to create something as iconic as this for the NO campaign? . . . If yes, get in touch." The 1984 advertisement was not the only reference to Steve Jobs – another of Cummings's heroes – in the post. He quoted Jobs: "Let's make it simple. Really simple." To win, Cummings argued, "Everything will need to be pared down to a few fundamental objectives such as: neutralising fear of NO, explaining the gains from regaining control, explaining the costs and dangers of continuing to give away control, and developing a feeling in the country that NO would not just be good for us but good for the world. It will also require avoiding using language that confuses. For example, the word 'sovereignty' is for many people 'something to do with the queen'. Stop using it."

Cummings's line of thinking on what strategy to pursue was closer to Banks's than either would want to admit. Both were aware of the traps that Eurosceptics had fallen into over the years and wanted to take a radically different approach. Specifically, they both, in their own ways, knew that Eurosceptics were all too comfortable working each other up over the finer points of EU trade policy when what they needed to do was, as Cummings put it, "break out of the ghetto". Yet, despite this common ground, attempts to bring Eurosceptics together were floundering, only a few months after pleasant emails arranging lunch at Shepherd's for a friendly discussion. In an email on 23 July, Banks told Cummings and Elliott:

> I don't feel you can move forward at the speed we can, given your diverse base of support. The "we must give the PM a chance" (yawn) line is too strong. I believe a non-political campaign has the maximum chance of being inclusive of all likely support groups.
>
> My initial reaction is a good Thatcher principle is let the market decide [sic], why don't we run side by side for the time being. For me this isn't about ego but about winning the vote.

A possible way forward would be for Dominic to come over to the know campaign [as Leave.EU was then called] [as] director, and get started on it in preparation for a merge of efforts in due course. When the time is right.

A week later, Banks told Stuart Wheeler and Lord Pearson that Elliott rejected the offer of eventually combining efforts: "He seems to want total control, which is hardly feasible." Elliott meanwhile had written to Wheeler denying that Banks had actually offered to merge efforts and merely asked him to consider how such an operation would work. He added: "Whilst we'd be happy to report to a Board, we would obviously have to have control over staffing. It's impossible to be in charge of something and not to have control over the operational side of things, otherwise you get factions and people start playing various Board members off against each other."

It must have been disheartening for Wheeler, a dedicated Eurosceptic, to find himself playing peacemaker between squabbling Leave factions with a referendum around the corner. At the end of July, he took stock of the deterioration in relations in an email to Elliott and Cummings. Under the subject line "STRICTLY PRIVATE & CONFIDENTIAL" he said he was "terribly sorry that Arron seems to be pushing ahead and criticising other Eurosceptics. It certainly does look as if there is very little chance of persuading him not to try to be the Electoral Commission chosen No [i.e. Leave] campaign leader or group. I think he is pretty unlikely to succeed."

A source of much of the tension between Banks and Elliott/Cummings was a suspicion that Elliott and Cummings were not committed to leaving the EU. As well as Cummings's flirtation with a second referendum, there was Elliott's ongoing involvement with Business for Britain, which was officially yet to deviate from its agnostic stance on EU membership. That summer, Business for Britain published *Change, or go*, a doorstopper report of nearly half a million words and more than a thousand pages, on "How Britain would gain influence and prosper outside an unreformed EU". Partly funded by a £250,000 grant from the Telegraph newspaper group, it described, according to Elliott in the report's executive summary, "which changes should be sought from renegotiation, and what the impact of a looser relationship with the EU would be on Britain" and it explained "how Britain is in a win-win situation as it seeks to agree a better deal with our fellow EU member states, and shows how remaining in an unreformed EU, given the push towards greater political integration, represents the worst of all worlds".

Change, or go covered four areas: why the EU needed to change, what those changes should be, how Britain would "gain influence outside an unreformed EU", and finally how it would prosper if it left. Under "The Change We Need", its authors argued for an end to ever closer union, repatriation of control over social and employment laws, an end to free movement of labour, and a restoration of Britain's veto over EU laws. In other words, Business for Britain made demands Cameron would never make himself, let alone hope to deliver in Brussels. In arguing that such reforms would be so fundamental that treaty change would be required, *Change, or go* echoed ExCom's initial statement, in which Leave MPs had said that Cameron could only keep his Bloomberg promise by making similarly substantial changes to Britain's relationship with the EU. In other words, even those unfamiliar with the tactics of those behind the report could see that Business for Britain was more interested in "go" than "change".

If the Banks camp's reservations about Elliott and Cummings centred on their reluctance to shed Business for Britain's hazy stance on Brexit and launch a full-blooded Out campaign as well as their flirtation with the idea of a second referendum, then Elliott and Co's suspicions concerned on one man and the role he would play in the vote. Few denied that Nigel Farage deserved much of the credit for securing a referendum. His populist movement had brought the Leave camp to the brink of finally having a say on EU membership, yet as the referendum drew nearer, many remained worried about the Farage Paradox, the idea that as the UKIP leader's profile rose, support for Leave fell.

The lesson non-UKIP Brexiteers took from that correlation was that Farage's role in the campaign would need to be limited, or at least in some sense sealed off from the official Leave campaign; otherwise he would put off too many undecided voters. To UKIP backers and politicians, this analysis was anathema to everything they had learned in the UKIP surge of the previous few years. They watched Farage pull in crowds across the country, marvelled at his ability to get along with whomever he spoke to, and credited him with leading arguably the most remarkable insurgency in modern British political history. The disagreement over how to involve

Farage in the campaign was so intractable because both sides had a point. Farage undoubtedly had a magnetism that outshone most politicians. But he has always been a Marmite politician, provoking strong reactions both positive and negative. The Westminster Leavers were eager to point out the difference between inspiring devotion from 15 per cent of the electorate and winning round 50 per cent plus one to their point of view. Cummings stressed this in an email to Wheeler who, though a UKIP donor, backed the Elliott camp: "Arron wants to run this campaign" and "he wants to make Farage the main spokesman which would be fatal." Neither side was going to budge on the Farage question.

By September, prospects of the Brexit coalition working together looked even bleaker. On 4 September, Arron Banks forwarded to Malcolm Pearson a message from an unnamed correspondent. The message was titled "BRIEFING: QUESTIONS MATTHEW ELLIOTT DOESN'T WANT TO ANSWER". It claimed Elliott had made clumsy accounting mistakes with Business for Britain, omitting to declare £115,000 of income. It pointed out that Elliott had a potential conflict of interest in running a national campaign while he had a commercial interest in a data company called WESS Digital, asking: "Would you see it as a fair use of people's data when they sign up to single issue, non-profit campaigns – such as a referendum campaign perhaps – if their details are sold for profit on to political parties to utilise during elections?" It also queried whether or not there was a further conflict of interest in Elliott having "evident ambitions to monitor, record market and profit from data" while chairing Big Brother Watch, an anti-surveillance campaign organisation. The anonymous author went on to question Elliott's credibility as a campaigner – specifically the success of No to AV – and the sincerity of his Euroscepticism, based on Business for Britain's ambiguity on membership. This, the message argued, would jeopardise his designation bid: "Doesn't your personal history of campaigning for renegotiation and staying in the EU . . . mean the Electoral Commission is highly unlikely to appoint an 'out' campaign that you run?" The anonymous author's final "question" was: "Aren't you just a low-grade political entrepreneur trying opportunistically to get a slice of this significant event and the benefits that will entail for you financially?"

Just a few days later, what had already been an unexpectedly tumultuous 2015 took a turn for the bizarre when Banks emailed Cummings and

Elliott: "Thought I would drop you a line. I'm aware that I have a personal investigator on my tail. The heat is obviously rising in the kitchen!! You might want to watch out – I have a business that specialises in personal security and counter intelligence and if need any help shout . . . It's almost certainly going to be a very dirty war . . . Arron. Ps I hope you are thinking of coming together because together we are stronger!"

With Banks's Leave.EU breathing down their necks, Elliott's team had to ditch the "change or go" strategy that would have meant only coming out for Leave much later in the day, after Cameron had unveiled a renegotiation package that inevitably failed to meet Business for Britain's deliberately very high standards. Even those who supported the Elliott campaign worried they were leaving it late. Wheeler emailed Cummings and Elliott on 5 October: "We have got going much too late . . . here we are in October with Arron having recruited some extremely important backers."

Instead, Vote Leave, the organisation they would ultimately submit for official designation, launched in early October. There was no event to mark the occasion; it was simply a case of voteleavetakecontrol.org going live. One Vote Leave insider described to us a panicked launch of the website, with senior members of the team being given very little time to see it before it went live. Some were surprised to find a mention of a second referendum, not something they had known was part of their strategy. "I thought I was working for a Leave campaign," said one Vote Leave staff member.

By now the split between the Leave camps was out in the open. The In campaign's deputy director, Lucy Thomas, responded to the launch dismissively, saying the "various competing Out campaigners have spent all summer fighting. They can't even bear to be in the same room as each other, let alone agree what life outside Europe would really look like for Britain."

Banks seemed to confirm his opponents' characterisation of the state of relations between Leave.EU and Vote Leave in an email to Elliott two days after Vote Leave had launched. He wrote: "The website is awful, the Facebook page worse . . . You may know politics, but have ABSOLUTELY no clue how to reach out to a wider audience . . . If this is your best shot, you should be shot . . . for goodness sake get a grip."

***

As if fighting between the two groups wasn't enough of a distraction, disharmony within Vote Leave was also becoming a problem by late 2015. In November, Richard Murphy, who had been recruited by Elliott to run Vote Leave's ground campaign, walked out. Murphy, who had worked as a campaign strategist for the Conservative Party for 18 years, described to us the "supreme lack of interest" in the ground campaign at Vote Leave. He said that his conversations with Cummings in particular demonstrated that the strategist lacked the interest in the nuts and bolts of a campaign that would make a difference on the ground. In one conversation about street stalls at Vote Leave, Cummings suggested charging volunteers for the privilege of manning them. Murphy's despondency had set in earlier when, he says, Cummings asked him whether a voter needed to go to a specific polling station or whether he or she could vote anywhere.

Others had more general complaints: about Cummings's ever-growing but never properly identified role in the campaign, about an unhappy working environment, about a management team seemingly allergic to being asked difficult questions, whether they came from Vote Leave board members or members of staff.

Problems at Vote Leave continued to pile up. Peter Bone and Tom Pursglove, neighbouring Northamptonshire MPs who had been signed up to Steve Baker's Conservatives for Britain, the parliamentary Conservative Leave group affiliated with Vote Leave, were invited to discuss the ground war in the referendum. Bone had spent much of the general election campaigning with Pursglove in Corby where they overturned a Labour majority of nearly 8,000 with a campaign largely detached from the national Conservative effort and focusing on the twin issues of EU membership and immigration. In a meeting with, among other people, Cummings, Bone criticised the NHS messaging and the unauthorised use of the NHS logo on a Vote Leave leaflet. He pointed out that he and other Conservative MPs would rather not hand out leaflets that implied the Conservative government was failing the health service. According to a Vote Leave board member present at the meeting, Cummings did not take the criticisms well, responding intemperately to Bone's point. When a second area of difference opened up between Bone and Cummings – this time over how to respond to the Prime Minister not ruling out leading the Leave campaign if he did not get the renegotiation he wanted – Bone walked out.

He and Pursglove, who also had his doubts about the Vote Leave operation, were dedicated Eurosceptics keen to work for a Leave vote whether or not it was with Cummings and Elliott. Instead of working with Vote Leave, they resolved to "do what we knew best", as Bone put it to us. "We decided to set up an organisation to campaign on a local level," he said, "knocking on doors and distributing leaflets." In December, they founded Grassroots Out, announcing themselves with a garish fluorescent green and black colour scheme. (Bone's bright tie was a permanent presence on the campaign trail.) Richard Murphy, who signed up with Leave.EU after departing from Vote Leave, also lent his time to Pursglove and Bone's operation. "The idea," Murphy said, "was to do the boring bit. We would find Tory MPs who were happy for us to set up a ground campaign in their constituency." And so the Leave landscape grew even more complicated.

As the Vote Leave operation grew in late 2015, gearing up for the referendum they now knew was likely to take place the following summer, patterns of decision-making started to emerge that troubled not only members of staff but also senior board members. One Vote Leave employee described to us the way in which Cummings's responsibilities appeared to grow even though he was supposedly there only to give advice and help Elliott get the operation off the ground. Instead, he was bringing in his own team, giving them responsibility for important parts of the campaign, chairing meetings and deciding important messaging questions. While there were advantages to having a small group making the important decisions in such a campaign, one board member told us of his concerns that there was a "determination from Dominic to be completely unaccountable".

These concerns came to a head after a November speech to the CBI by Cameron was interrupted by two students who heckled the Prime Minister and held up a sign that read "CBI = VOICE OF BRUSSELS". Vote Leave board members, who knew nothing of the publicity stunt until after it had happened, were shocked to learn that it had in fact been facilitated by their organisation. Vote Leave staff had set up "Lyon Sheppard Web Solutions" as a website and registered it as a company so that the students could gain entry to the event as directors of a business. The incident marked a considerable escalation in the hostility from Vote Leave towards the Prime Minister, something Conservative politicians on the board were understandably sensitive about.

The CBI stunt left a long wake in terms of internal Vote Leave relations. For one senior Conservative, his relationship with Cummings never recovered from that moment, and by January there was a move from the board to sack him. Exactly why "Domfall" (as one insider jokingly referred to it) failed is not entirely clear. A group of board members, led by Bernard Jenkin and at odds with Cummings over his attacks on the Prime Minister and the sour taste he left with many members of the Vote Leave staff, sought to push him out and planned to do so by offering him a demotion (even though at the time he had no contract or properly defined role) he would refuse to accept. Unfortunately for Jenkin, Cummings got wind of the move against him before the meeting. According to one board member, at what was supposed to be the meeting at which Cummings was ousted, he raised the issue of a lawyer's letter sent on behalf of Arron Banks to Jenkin and the board concerning "casual smears" made against Banks and Farage. Debate over this question, as well as Cummings mobilising support on the board and among Vote Leave staff, appears to have distracted the board from the meeting's original purpose. Although Cummings came "ludicrously close" to losing his job on more than one occasion, the board member told us, calling that particular board meeting "farcical", Domfall never happened.

Looking back on the attempted ousting after the vote, Bernard Jenkin described the dispute as "hugely draining of energy and momentum, which was painful and frustrating for everyone." He insists, however, that the outcome was "positive":

> The result was that we established proper governance and the authority of the board over the campaign. This was hugely important for Vote Leave's reputation with donors and with the Electoral Commission. The board was still too big to function effectively as a whole, so it relied very heavily on the Chairman (Nigel Lawson and then Gisela Stuart); the compliance committee chairman Daniel Hodson, the chairman of the finance committee, Jon Moynihan, and the designated "Responsible Person", Alan Halsall.

By early 2016, the failure to build a well-oiled Brexit coalition had faded from the minds of those involved in the referendum campaign. Many felt they had been worrying for too long about whether or not Cummings and

Banks would get along. Soon they would have an answer to a much more important question, one that would play a far bigger part in whether or not the UK left the European Union: could David Cameron get the deal he so badly needed from Brussels? ℰ

David Cameron and Donald Tusk pictured during the Prime Minister's all-important renegotiation summit. The Prime Minister's disappointing reforms were poorly received by the British press and electorate.

Picture by: Yves Herman/AP/Press Association Images

Chapter Four:
Best of Both Worlds?

The Conservative victory at the 2015 general election defied the polls, confounded the pundits and brought tears to the Prime Minister's eyes. In a stump speech delivered a week before polling day, Cameron described the vote as "career-defining". In hindsight the general election was really the second in a series of three career-defining (i.e. potentially career-ending) votes in three years.

In 2014, Cameron dodged becoming the Prime Minister who lost Scotland. In 2015, he avoided joining that unfashionable club of Prime Ministers who never won an election. "By the end of 2017", as the Conservatives had promised in a manifesto they never expected to be in a position fully to deliver, he would find out if he was to become the Prime Minister ignored by the British people on the question of European membership.

The referendum pledge, a promise made at a political low ebb, transformed what could have been a year reaping the benefits of an election that had delivered a Conservative majority, badly wounded Labour and revealed UKIP to be both very bad at winning seats in the House of Commons and as much a threat to Labour as to the Conservatives. But the leader who in 2006 had warned his party against "banging on" about Europe had what should have been his finest hour dominated by the issue. Cameron delivered speeches on an ambitious domestic agenda, setting out solutions to big problems like poverty and extremism. In October, the Prime Minister appeared to break new ground at the Conservative party conference when he was applauded for raising the iniquity of a black woman having to change her name to Elizabeth to get a job interview. (Looking back, that moment may have been the high-water mark of Tory modernisation.) But the tick-tock of the referendum countdown was impossible for Cameron to ignore.

By his own logic, referendum victory depended on a renegotiation substantial enough for the EU to be worth staying in. He avoided saying the UK was better off as a member of the EU per se. The preferred phrase, a phrase that British voters would come to hear day after day for the 13 months between general election and referendum, was "better off in a *reformed* Europe".

On November 10, 2015, the Prime Minister fleshed out what he had meant by a "new settlement" nearly three years earlier in the Bloomberg speech. At Chatham House, Cameron revealed "four objectives at the heart of my renegotiation":

> Objective one: protect the single market for Britain and others outside the eurozone. What I mean by that is a set of binding principles that guarantee fairness between euro and non-euro countries.
>
> Objective two: write competitiveness into the DNA of the whole European Union. And this includes cutting the total burden on business.
>
> Objective three: exempt Britain from an "ever closer union" and bolster national parliaments. Not through warm words but through legally binding and irreversible changes.
>
> And objective four: tackle abuses of the right to free movement, and enable us to control migration from the European Union, in line with our manifesto.
>
> The precise form all these changes will take will be a matter for the renegotiation. But I want to be very clear: if we are able to reach agreement, it must be on a basis that is legally-binding and irreversible and where necessary has force in the treaties.

He went on: "Those who say Britain should stay in the EU at all costs need to explain why Britain should accept the status quo. I am clear that there are real problems for Britain with the status quo. There are some economic risks . . . And there are also significant risks if we allow our sovereignty to be eroded by ever closer union or sit by and do nothing about the unsustainable rate of migration to our country." Cameron also wrote to Donald Tusk, President of the European Council, outlining these demands as a "starting point" for negotiations (though of course, in reality, these "initial demands" were themselves the result of extensive talks).

A year earlier, discussing the reforms he wanted to see to free movement of labour, Cameron said: "If our concerns fall on deaf ears and we cannot put our relationship with the EU on a better footing, then of course I rule nothing out." Such Eurosceptic proclamations seem odd coming from the man who would go on to lead the campaign to keep the UK in the EU. Their most simple explanation is that Cameron is a Eurosceptic. He may have dismissed UKIP as a "bunch of fruitcakes, loonies and closet racists", he may have tried to steer his party away from the European rocks on which so many of his predecessors had been wrecked, but before the referendum campaign it would be difficult to say he had shown any enthusiasm for the European project.

Ahead of the 2001 general election, when he was Conservative candidate for the vacant safe seat of Witney in Oxfordshire, Cameron had a question mark next to his name on libertarian pamphleteer Sean Gabb's influential "Candidlist", which classified hundreds of Tory candidates as either Europhile or Eurosceptic. According to *Call Me Dave*, a biography by Lord Ashcroft and Isabel Oakeshott, Cameron took issue with the question mark in an email to Gabb, arguing he should be classified as Eurosceptic "on the basis that I oppose the single currency and any further transfer of sovereignty from the UK to the EU". In a second email he said "these are my views – no to the single currency, no to further transfer of powers from Westminster to Brussels and yes to renegotiation of areas like Fish where the EU has been a disaster for the UK. If that is being a Europhile, then I'm a banana." As a newly-elected MP he kept a blog for the *Guardian* on which he described Tony Blair as a "Euromaniac" and, sounding like a Boris Johnson tribute act, lampooned "Euro-puddings" and "Euro-farce".

Cameron's sceptical appeal for reform may have been sincere, but in late 2015 it was also a tactical necessity. He found himself in a paradoxical bind in the build-up to the referendum: in order to secure a renegotiation that would deliver the Remain vote he wanted, he had to persuade European leaders he was willing to leave. Compounding this paradox was the prospect of the Prime Minister having to switch from this vocal Euroscepticism to Euro-enthusiasm in a manner that seemed convincing to voters. The political calculation was straightforward: the more substantial the renegotiation, the easier the about-turn Cameron would have to pull off once he had a deal.

A December 2015 Survation poll of more than 7,000 people – a considerable sample size – conducted privately for UKIP confirmed the importance of the renegotiation to the referendum. Voters fell into three groups of roughly the same size. A third said they would vote Leave no matter what Cameron achieved in his renegotiations, a third said they would vote Remain come what may, while a third said they would consider switching their vote based on the outcome of the renegotiation. In other words, Cameron's survival depended on achieving a renegotiation he could sell to the British people.

Cameron's diplomatic campaign for European reform did not begin in 2015. Even before he had delivered the Bloomberg speech, he was making the case for change to continental leaders. As early as November 2012, he was pressing for a comprehensive package of reforms. A Downing Street dinner was the setting for a significant and telling exchange with Angela Merkel on the future of Britain and the EU. Asked by Merkel why the British had grown so frustrated with the EU, Cameron pointed to the single currency and the ongoing eurozone crisis, which, he argued, was being prioritised to the detriment of non-eurozone member states and the single market generally. Cameron's second explanation for British discontent was that "the British people never got a choice to vote on Lisbon. It spread much unhappiness towards the political establishment." According to Anthony Seldon and Peter Snowdon's *Cameron at 10*, in which the evening is recounted in detail, when asked by Merkel whether he supported EU membership, the Prime Minister replied:

> Like many in my party, I've supported our membership of the EU all my political life, but I am worried that if I don't get the reform objectives I'm setting out, I won't be able to keep Britain in. I am passionate about the single market, I am passionate about foreign policy co-operation, but if I don't listen to British public opinion, then Britain will depart from Europe. The European project was mis-sold here, so what I want are changes that will make it possible for Britain to stay in.

Later in their discussion, Merkel said to Cameron that Britain leaving the EU could be fatal for the project: "Without you, I don't know what is going to happen." Cameron went on to plead with Merkel about the importance of reform to the case for Remain: "I need to make a pitch to the country. If there is no acceptable deal, it's not the end of the world. I'll walk away from the EU."

The lesson Cameron's aides, in particular his Chief of Staff Ed Llewellyn, took from the dinner was that to stand a chance of succeeding in a Brussels renegotiation, the Prime Minister would have to make it an argument about broader European reform. The Eurosceptics that Cameron had hoped to bring on board, however, had little interest in reform of Europe in general. Their focus was overwhelmingly on securing a better deal for Britain, not the future of an institution most of them had already lost faith in. Bernard Jenkin spoke for many Eurosceptic backbenchers when he told us that Cameron made a "fatal mistake when he made it about Europe" as Merkel had suggested. This was as much a difference of perspective as it was a difference of opinion and, though unsurprising, it demonstrated the tightrope Cameron would have to walk for his renegotiations to be a success: his home audience was hungry for a deal that secured "special status" for the UK; meanwhile, he knew he would not get very far with his European counterparts by simply seeking concessions for Britain.

Cameron's task was all the more daunting for the complex series of overlapping and conflicting allegiances he would have to navigate in Europe's corridors of power. Throughout the process he knew he could rely on Ireland, Sweden, Denmark and the Netherlands, countries who shared British concerns about the EU, or had a lot to lose from the UK leaving, or both. Beyond that group, however, the strength of alliance depended on the issue in question: new member states in Eastern Europe agreed wholeheartedly with Cameron's single-market anti-regulation drive but stood staunchly opposed to compromise on the absolute free movement of people. Southern states, being integrationist by instinct, were generally suspicious of any reforms that might undermine the strength of the eurozone.

After the first summit of EU leaders since the general election Cameron admitted that the process would take "patience and tenacity" and that he had not been met by a "wall of love" from his counterparts. One key ingredient in his recipe for renegotiation success was air miles. Early on in his premiership, he had focused his European diplomacy on Angela Merkel, often to the exclusion of other leaders. Such a strategy had failed spectacularly when Cameron had fought in vain to block Jean-Claude Juncker's appointment as President of the European Commission. To secure meaningful reforms he would have to reach out beyond the European leader whom he knew best and with whom he was said to have such good chemistry that one aide described their phone calls as "almost flirtatious".

By the beginning of the summer, Cameron's European charm offensive was in full swing. During one 48-hour tour he visited François Hollande in Paris, Merkel in Berlin, Dutch Prime Minister Mark Rutte in The Hague and Polish premier Ewa Kopacz in Warsaw. Later in the year he became the first British PM to visit Austria in 34 years when he met Chancellor Werner Faymann in Vienna. Other visits took Cameron further afield, including to Vilnius, Sofia and Bucharest. One official told the *Financial Times* he thought Cameron's renegotiation push meant he had visited more European capitals than any other Prime Minister.

The product of Cameron's efforts, released as a draft proposal in a letter from Donald Tusk to European leaders on 2 February, was to be – after a final diplomatic push from the Prime Minister – finalised and agreed on when European leaders met later in the month. The day on which Cameron needed to secure an agreement he could sell to the British people started with several of his European counterparts, most notably Hollande, expressing major reservations about the package Tusk and Cameron had proposed. Going into the final talks, one Number Ten source was quoted as saying, "This is going to be tough. This is going to be a long night." There remained numerous significant sticking points: Cameron's proposal on curbing benefits for EU migrants remained highly contentious and the nature of the UK's opt-out from "ever closer union" still could not be settled. The Downing Street source was right; at 5.30 the following morning, Cameron left talks with Juncker and Tusk, refusing to comment on the prospects of a deal on his way out. Talks resumed at 9.30 a.m. and at 9.30 p.m. the world knew agreement had been reached, thanks to Tusk's Twitter account: "Deal. Unanimous support for new settlement for #UKinEU."

Brussels convention stipulates that the first post-summit press conference is held by the European Council President and the President of the European Commission, but this time, as leaders emerged from their several-stage marathon negotiation, Cameron was given the top billing before Europe's media. The whole continent may have been listening to the Prime Minister, but after months of pressing the flesh Cameron's comments were designed not just for Britain but for the Eurosceptic but risk-averse middle third of the electorate who he knew would decide the result of the forthcoming referendum. As soon as agreement had been reached, he needed to change from diplomat to campaigner, from negotiator to salesman. And the sales pitch began immediately. "This deal," he told the press, "has delivered on the commitments I made at the beginning of the renegotiation process . . . I believe this is enough for me to recommend that the United Kingdom remain in the European Union." He claimed the deal secured a "special status" that offered "the best of both worlds", exempt from the aspects of the EU that did not work for Britain, influencing decisions in areas that did.

In his foreword to *The best of both worlds: the United Kingdom's special status in a reformed European Union*, the government document explaining the package of reforms, Cameron emphasised his sceptical, pragmatic case for membership: "Mine is a hard-headed assessment of what is in our best interests, not driven by some emotional attachment. I have certainly had my doubts about the European Union as an organisation and I still do."

The document boasted that the settlement achieved by Cameron "secured all the UK's objectives". Dividing the reforms package into the four areas Cameron had outlined in his November speech, the document claimed that the "settlement makes the EU work much better for the UK" but that "the task of reforming the EU does not end with today's agreement".

On economic governance, Cameron claimed to have kept the pound and ensured that UK businesses could not be discriminated against because the UK was not in the eurozone, and that the UK taxpayer would not have to pay for eurozone bail-outs. The reforms also introduced a means of recourse for member states concerned that such principles had not been honoured: they could flag an issue for further discussion. The former promises on economic governance may have given Cameron some clear lines – "we will never join the euro" – but did little to placate those who thought that battle had been fought – and won – already. More significant, and widely seen as a significant win for the Prime Minister, was the latter proposal, in that it gave a single non-eurozone leader the power to bring eurozone actions to a halt.

On competitiveness, Cameron's second area for reform, the government boasted of a "firm commitment" to drive harder at a pre-existing agenda of economic reform, which would reduce red tape, bring down barriers to trade within the EU and pursue "with renewed commitment" trade agreements with other economies. Competitiveness was undoubtedly the lowest-hanging fruit of the renegotiation, mostly because the agreement in this area was inconsequential, amounting to nothing more than vague commitments that went no further than what had already been agreed upon by European leaders. Implementation, not good intentions, is what matters when it comes to trade deals and cutting red tape, and the agreement showed little evidence of anything more than meaning well. The government document's use of language such as "drive harder" and "ambitious agenda" served as a thin veil to conceal the lack of concrete changes.

Sovereignty – for many Eurosceptics, the red-hot core of why they would be voting Leave – was always going to be a vital area of the renegotiation. In November Cameron had called for a British exemption from an "ever closer union" and for a bolstering of national parliaments "not through warm words but through legally binding and irreversible changes". Cameron would not have committed to such a clear-cut and central exemption on "ever closer union" – the three words that had come to stand for the ratcheting federalisation that summed up all that Leavers thought was wrong with the EU – had he not been confident, or in fact assured, of delivering it. The deal "recognised that the UK is not committed to further political integration into the European Union" and pledged to incorporate this into the EU Treaties when they were next revised. Given that the reform package was touted as securing a new, "best of both worlds" relationship between the UK and the rest of the EU, it is notable that the exemption from ever closer union was a recognition of the status quo rather than a change.

Cameron's deal did bolster national parliaments, introducing a red card procedure by which they could combine to block unwanted EU legislation whereas before they were only able to force a review of the legislation in question. But the bar for such a move was set at an all but impossible to reach 55 per cent of national parliaments (or 16 parliaments in the current 28-member EU) and was limited to issues of subsidiarity. In that sense, the red card provision had much in common with other aspects of the reform package: heavy on symbolic value, light on utility. This is hardly a surprise given that the reforms were sought with a referendum in mind and that what mattered to British voters, and therefore to Cameron, was unlikely to be the detail of the changes. Instead, Cameron appeared to have started with a soundbite and then reverse-engineered a reform to match it that was inconsequential enough for unsympathetic European leaders to agree to.

The Conservative government's unfulfilled pledge to bring annual net migration to below 100,000 a year, reaffirmed ahead of the general election, had made more conspicuous than ever the powerlessness of a national government to have the final say on flows into the country while it was a member of the EU. As public concern about the issue grew, so too did support for UKIP, while complacency on the subject eroded public trust in mainstream political parties. Cameron had emphasised the importance of migration to his renegotiation early on, identifying free movement of people as the pillar of the European Union that caused the most noticeable disquiet among British voters. The Conservatives fought the general election with a manifesto promising to make "changes to welfare to cut EU migration an absolute requirement in the renegotiation", specifically pledging to "insist that EU migrants who want to claim tax credits and child benefits must live here and contribute to our country for a minimum of four years" as a way of "reducing the financial incentive for lower-paid, lower-skilled workers to come to Britain". As Cameron had put it in his November speech, the overarching objective on migration was to "tackle abuses of the right to free movement, and enable us to control migration from the European Union".

What did Cameron get on the all-important migration question? Instead of the four-year wait for EU migrants to claim in-work benefits promised in the Conservative manifesto, the agreement offered an emergency brake under which the UK could phase in access to in-work benefits over four years. This would kick in immediately but would only last for seven years, at which point the brake would lapse. The UK could ask to apply the brake again but the final decision would be the Commission's. Cameron had wanted a ban on child benefit payments for children living abroad. This was not agreed to; instead, such payments could be indexed to the cost of living in the country where the recipient's child lived. Both the emergency brake and the change to child benefits had to be put forward as legislation in the European Parliament, meaning these compromises were not even guaranteed.

There are two ways to assess Cameron's renegotiation. The most straightforward measure – how much of what he asked for did he get? – fails to take account of the staged nature of his demands, themselves the product of substantial discussion with other member states. The real question Cameron needed to answer – the question on the minds of many British voters – was how much these reforms really changed. Was the package so transformative that its contents delivered the "best of both worlds", as Cameron claimed?

"Call that a deal, Dave?" roared that Saturday's *Daily Mail* front page. The Telegraph's leader argued that "the events of the past few days" only proved that "the EU is arcane and sclerotic" before looking forward and calling on both pro-EU and Brexit activists to "rise to the occasion, offering a campaign rooted in facts and reason rather than fearmongering". Even *The Times*, which would go on to endorse Remain in the Referendum, called Cameron's deal "thin gruel", arguing he had gone to the land of chocolate and brought back a fudge: "A live-and-let-live Europe is what Cameron promised along with a referendum. His problem, and Britain's, is that he has not delivered it."

Cameron returned not only to a hostile press but to an electorate two thirds of which had wanted to see a transfer of powers from Brussels to Westminster, and which would struggle to find any meaningful repatriation of powers in his deal. The ultimate verdict on the renegotiation came from Cameron himself in the form of the scant mention he gave the details of his reforms on the campaign trail in the months ahead. He would talk of a *reformed* Europe but those reforms were generally brushed over by those making the case for Remain. In other words, there was a reform-shaped hole in the case for Remain that voters would come to hear.

Meanwhile, the deal could hardly have slotted into the "change or go" logic of Vote Leave more neatly. Yes, the Prime Minister could have come away with less, but the claim that the status quo had changed such that the UK had a new "special status" that gave the British the best of both worlds was a long way from the truth. For wavering voters sceptical of the EU's adaptability to the problems it faced or its consideration for the concerns of the British people, Cameron and his counterparts' months of bargaining confirmed their worst suspicions about the European Union.

Over those months, with Cameron having enforced a restriction on cabinet ministers coming out for Leave until after the renegotiation was finished and he had presented it to the cabinet, mildly wavering Eurosceptic Conservative backbenchers had bought in to the spirit of this truce. "How will you be voting in the referendum?" they were asked throughout 2015 and early 2016. "Let's see how the Prime Minister's renegotiation goes," came the response from a great many of them. And so, inadvertently, Cameron's truce raised the stakes of his renegotiation.

MPs' calls for patience only made the renegotiation a bigger factor in their stance on EU membership. Among Conservative backbenchers, the numbers spoke for themselves. Many had expected around 50 Conservatives to come out for Leave. The final tally was 138.

Could Cameron have got a better deal? Some Tories certainly believed so. Hannan, for example, put the argument to us that if Cameron had made the renegotiation less about migration and more about sovereignty and the return of powers, he could have gained significant concessions. Denmark had important rights returned to it in these areas after it rejected Maastricht in its first referendum. In Hannan's view Cameron did not push these issues as they were simply of little interest to him – and that is why he lost the referendum: "If Cameron had delivered what he had promised at Bloomberg, which was a proper overhaul and the return of powers, he'd have won. I don't think there's much doubt about that." Hannan's assessment, however, depends on an unrealistically optimistic view of other member states' willingness to offer concessions on sovereignty.

At a lectern in front of Number Ten – the mark of an Important Moment in British politics these days – Cameron, having hosted the cabinet meeting after which ministers would be free to campaign for Leave, told the country: "I do not love Brussels, I love Britain. I am the first to say that there are still many ways in which Europe needs to improve and that the task of reforming Europe does not end with yesterday's agreement." Announcing the date of the referendum, 23 June, he said his view was clear: "Britain will be stronger, safer and better off in a reformed European Union."

For Leave campaigners, this announcement was tantamount to the starting gun of the referendum fight. Moments after Cameron had finished speaking, six cabinet members came out for Leave. In an amateurishly staged photocall in a corner of the Vote Leave offices, surrounded by volunteers in red T-shirts waving Vote Leave placards, Priti Patel, Iain Duncan Smith, Chris Grayling, John Whittingdale, Theresa Villiers and Michael Gove posed for the press. The six ministers had signed and were holding a banner emblazoned with words the British public would grow familiar with over the coming months: "Let's take back control." The most important name on that list, and for Cameron the one that hurt the most, was Gove. The diehard Cameroon published a 1,500-word statement explaining his move. "For weeks now I have been wrestling with the most difficult decision of my political life," wrote the Justice Secretary, "but taking difficult decisions is what politicians are paid to do . . . I was encouraged to stand for Parliament by David Cameron and he has given me the opportunity to serve in what I believe is a great, reforming government. I think he is an outstanding Prime Minister. There is, as far as I can see, only one significant issue on which we have differed. And that is the future of the UK in the European Union."

That weekend, there was one more politician the country was waiting to hear from. Boris Johnson was not just the most popular politician in the country but an out-and-out celebrity with a frequently inexplicable capacity to cut across the usual political dividing lines. On Sunday afternoon he emerged from his Islington home, where a scrum of cameramen, journalists and baffled onlookers was waiting for him. Just a matter of minutes after texting the Prime Minister with his decision on which side he would back in the referendum, he spoke to the cameras. Evaluating the renegotiation, he said: "I think everyone should pay tribute to David Cameron for what he pulled off in a very short space of time, but I don't think anybody could realistically claim that this is fundamental reform of the EU or of Britain's relationship with the EU." Johnson's statement was delicately worded. He went on: "I would like to see a new relationship based more on trade, on co-operation, but as I say with much less of this supranational element." For that reason he would be backing Vote Leave "or whatever the team is called". Amid the significant boost for the Leave camp, who would unanimously describe Boris as a decisive factor after the June result, few paid close attention to what he had said, or rather what he had chosen not to say. He had mentioned better deals and new relationships but at no point did the man who would go on to lead the Leave campaign actually say he wanted the UK out of the EU. *

From left, Peter Bone, Nigel Farage and George Galloway on stage at the launch of the Go Movement. The organisation challenged Vote Leave for designation.

Picture by: Isabel Infantes/EMPICS Entertainment

Chapter Five:
A Six-Week Slagging Match

Vote Leave campaigners could hardly have hoped for the crucial weekend in late February to have gone better. They had nothing to fear in Cameron's reform package, which was announced to a tepid reception in the press. They had secured the support of a credible bevy of cabinet ministers (though they were disappointed not to have Sajid Javid on board). Above all, though, they had Boris Johnson, a mercurial but charismatic figure whose support would boost the popularity of any political campaign.

Yet there remained a significant frustration, namely that the escalation of hostilities between Leave and Remain after Cameron's renegotiation had not stopped infighting within the Leave camp. Adamant that they would contest designation but aware that they alone would struggle to defeat Vote Leave on the criteria outlined by the Electoral Commission, Vote Leave's rivals – foremost among them Leave.EU and Grassroots Out – decided to morph into a new coalition, the GO Movement (with GO standing for Grassroots Out), which was launched at a disorganised but energetic and well-attended rally in Westminster's QEII conference centre on the day the renegotiation finished.

Peter Bone traces the GO Movement's inception to a Grassroots Out rally in Manchester in early February, at which Nigel Farage spoke. "It was clear by Manchester," he told us, "that Vote Leave and Leave.EU would never merge. Somebody came up with the bright idea of, what if there was an umbrella organisation which everyone is under?" It would have "individual pillars so their independence is protected and there would be a structure at the top called 'GO'." Though there was technically a berth available for Vote Leave in the GO Movement structure, there was little prospect of them taking it. If the speakers at the GO Movement's Westminster launch had one thing in common other than wanting to leave the EU, it was exasperation at Matthew Elliott or Dominic Cummings or both. Among those who addressed the standing-room-only hall were Conservatives Peter Bone, Tom Pursglove and Bill Cash, free-market economist Ruth Lea, Labour's Kate Hoey, the DUP's Sammy Wilson and UKIP's Farage.

Kate Hoey's characterisation of GO offers a sense of how they would seek to differentiate themselves from the comparatively narrow Vote Leave in front of the public and the Electoral Commission. She told the crowd, "There is a huge Eurosceptic movement in the United Kingdom", adding: "The GO Movement will act as an umbrella organisation to unite and mobilise." It would be "the people's campaign", she said. "We will take on the establishment and win this referendum to secure a better, safer and freer future for our country outside the EU."

Farage knew that for GO to have a chance of winning designation, a result that would make him the public face of the Leave movement, he and Banks needed to demonstrate that their organisation had a broader support base than Vote Leave and had to appear more willing to represent other Leave groups than Vote Leave. This was the reasoning behind the choice of the GO rally's "surprise guest" that Friday night. Introduced by Farage as a "towering figure", George Galloway walked down the central aisle of the hall, decked out in his trademark fedora and waistcoat. The Respect Party leader's presence prompted at least 100 attendees to walk out. But Farage saw short-term discontent as a price worth paying for having on their side a party not represented by Vote Leave. Later, Farage described to us the "amazing achievement" that was GO. It had "everything from the Traditional Unionist Voice in Northern Ireland to the official Communist Party of Britain," he said. "As a rainbow coalition, GO was an extraordinary thing."

The need to build a rainbow coalition explains signing Respect up as a GO member. It does not fully explain the prominence of Galloway as the much-hyped mystery guest. According to one senior GO campaigner, Galloway was an understudy for another, less contentious Brexiteer. As they put it to us, "You have to remember that we were hoping we were going to get a cabinet minister." Because the all-important Brussels summit had continued into a second day meaning the cabinet meeting after which ministers would be free to campaign did not take place until Saturday. And so Galloway was given top billing. One of the short-term consequences of inviting Galloway to the GO Movement launch was to give Vote Leave a powerful recruiting device. They could use his involvement to persuade Brexiteers with their feet in both camps that their campaign was the more palatable. Stronger In also made hay with a photograph of arguably the country's two most divisive politicians sporting matching Cheshire-cat grins: a vote for Leave was a vote for these men.

However determined both Vote Leave and Leave.EU, under the aegis of

GO, seemed in their pursuit of designation, some Leavers continued to push for a unified campaign. The week after the GO Movement launch, Lord Pearson circulated a message among senior Brexiteers. In it he wrote of his "fear that a battle for designation is looming, and that it may lose us the war, whichever side wins". Pearson and many like him feared that years fighting for an independent Britain would be squandered because of petty clashes between big personalities. "How can we fight a cohesive ten-week campaign after a six-week slagging match?" he asked, before attempting to clear the air between the various groups:

Let me start with the emergence of Arron Banks and his Leave EU initiative. I accept, and so does Arron, that some of his early emails were "unhelpful"; that he started the pillow fight in the nursery. But some of the slippers which came winging back, through press briefings, etc, were painful and equally inaccurate.

The slipper fight continued until Friday, January 29, when Richard Smith and I gave a private lunch for John Mills, Arron, Bill Cash and Richard Tice . . . Arron and Nigel [also present] repeated their offer of November [to merge] . . . John said he would put the offer to his board, which by Sunday 31 had rejected it again. So Richard Tice and Richard Smith went to see John in his office that Sunday evening and came up with the concept of an overarching "holding" company, The Leave Group (now the GO Movement), with a board of the "great and the good" from above the party fray, chaired by John, under which all groups would operate. John recommended this concept to his board on Tuesday 2nd February which rejected it.

I understand that fear of being too closely associated with UKIP may lie behind the rejection of any form of collaboration with Arron and Nigel. The conservative Euro-realist establishment believes that UKIP and Leave.EU are toxic with the crucial undecided voters, and wants to do its own thing with them. The GO Movement replies that this fear is exaggerated, that the "political class" is just as toxic with the key voters, and that Vote Leave and Conservatives for Britain personify this political class.

It seems to my co-signatories in the Lords, Richard Smith and me, that these positions should now be abandoned in the national interest. Nigel and Arron are still prepared to do this.

So this letter is a plea from all of us to sit round the table and agree a unified way forward which will secure the designation. The GO Movement appears to be the right sort of formula, with a revised board and everyone free to appeal to their most fruitful constituencies underneath it.

Malcolm Pearson's political instincts and past practice were strong clues as to why he was so adamant that the "warring groups must lift their eyes to victory". Made a Conservative peer in 1990 but a Eurosceptic from even earlier, Pearson had encouraged voters to back UKIP in the 2004 European elections, for which he was expelled from the Conservative Party. In 2007 he joined UKIP, becoming the party's leader in 2009 and calling for non-aggression pacts between UKIP and Eurosceptic Conservative MPs at the 2010 general election. Pearson, then, had always been keen to prioritise what he saw as the most important question in British politics – EU membership – over party politics.

If it was easy to see why Pearson, Bone and others were keen for more cooperation, it is also clear why Elliott and Cummings had no plans to work in any meaningful way with Leave.EU or under the GO umbrella. They still believed in the analysis they had bought into from the beginning – that a campaign that gave too much prominence to Farage was doomed to fail – and they remained confident that in a designation fight they would win Electoral Commission backing. A "six-week slagging match", to use Pearson's words, was, for Cummings and Elliott, a price worth paying for control over important campaign decisions such as who would appear in television debates and what Leave referendum broadcasts would look like. Above all, there was an obvious problem with the logic of the GO Movement: for subsidiaries of GO, independence could only go so far. Not for nothing was designation so desirable to referendum campaigners. As well as the higher spending limit, it meant control over who would appear in television debates; it meant deciding on the contents of the campaign's television broadcasts. However loose the GO coalition would be, its various factions would still have to reach an agreement on these questions. The original problem had not, therefore, been solved: the GO structure still meant Vote Leave and Leave.EU working together, something that was not going to happen.

**

With designation looming, Leave campaign fractures remained a theme of the campaign. The slagging match certainly did not stop, with missives flying back and forth on social media and in the press. Banks was fond of referring to Vote Leave's chief executive as "Lord Elliott of Loserville" while Vote Leave were by no means above briefing against Leave.EU, building a public picture of their rivals as an amateurish and volatile operation – not a wholly inaccurate picture. Thankfully though, both for the chances of a Leave victory and for the sanity of those following the Leave camp closely, most campaigners, whether they were at GO/Leave.EU or Vote Leave, spent March worrying about more important things than a war of words with other Brexiteers. By the end of the month they had to demonstrate as best they could that their organisation was the truest voice of the Leave side. By April 15, they would learn from the Electoral Commission whether or not they had been successful. Designation victory for Vote Leave meant sparing Matthew Elliott a career-ending flop of a campaign and securing control of the campaign for the most senior politicians involved. Designation for the GO Movement meant handing power over one side of the most important vote in a generation to an unpredictable and proudly outsider insurgency. After the referendum, Farage, who was in lockstep with Banks during the campaign, told us that he was "not always" happy with the tactics of his Bristolian backer and that there were "deficiencies" in terms of the "professional organisation" of Leave.EU.

While there was undoubtedly still internal unrest at Vote Leave's Westminster Tower headquarters, by March the organisation had set out their stall in terms of what their campaign would look like. Gisela Stuart, the German-born Labour MP who would be a prominent on-screen Leave campaigner during the campaign, took over from Nigel Lawson as chair of the organisation. The composition of a Campaign Committee was announced, with Stuart and Michael Gove as co-conveners. It also included Elliott and Cummings, with the latter's role now defined as Campaign Director. Fourteen of the 25 members were Conservatives, including senior figures such as Boris Johnson and Iain Duncan Smith, while four were from Labour. Then there was a smattering of other allegiances: Douglas Carswell from UKIP, Nigel Dodds from the DUP, former Labour and SDP MP Lord Owen, former Liberal Democrat MP Paul Keetch, and John Longworth, who had been Director-General of the British Chambers of Commerce until he was suspended by the organisation for his support for Brexit.

Vote Leave's designation bid would have been on much shakier ground had it not been for Douglas Carswell's presence. His endorsement of Vote Leave the previous year had enraged Banks and Farage, who saw a path to designation for themselves through blocking any UKIP support for Vote Leave. Without the support of a member of the biggest party that supported withdrawal, it would have been difficult for Vote Leave to claim they properly represented their side of the vote. This – as well as vicious enmity between Farage and Carswell – was the reasoning behind an unsuccessful attempt to suspend Carswell from the party ahead of the designation decision. It also explains Suzanne Evans, another supporter of Vote Leave, being sacked as UKIP's deputy chairwoman in February.

Vote Leave's application for designation boasted of 43,544 supporters, a grassroots campaign network and a series of Regional Business Councils set up by their "strategic partner" Business for Britain. Their application was full of pre-emptive rebuttals of their rival's pitch for designation, contrasting social media support – one of the GO Movement's strengths – with fully-signed-up and active Vote Leave supporters and volunteers. The application also painted Vote Leave as the safer pair of hands, arguing that "organisations capable of delivering an effective message to 46 million voters need to build on existing political structures and networks as well as creating new ones". Such an organisation "should be run by capable, experienced and responsible politicians and campaign professionals".

Much of Vote Leave's application would have been a surprising read to those familiar with what was a top-heavy, media-focused outfit. Describing Vote Leave as an "umbrella organisation", the application told of a belief in an approach that "embraces the widest possible range of opinion and appeals to the widest possible audience". The application made much of various "for Britain" organisations, business, academic and community campaign groups set up through Business for Britain that fell under the Vote Leave umbrella. As well as Lawyers for Britain, Historians for Britain and the City for Britain, there were Vapers for Britain, Muslims for Britain, Aussies for Britain, Farmers for Britain, BeLeave (the youth campaign for Leave), Out and Proud (LGBT Leave). While some of these groups really were active campaign organisations – for example, Hannan attributes Leave's strong performance in Birmingham to the work of Muslims for Britain campaigners – others were less active. An activist involved in the early days of Business for Britain described to us the way in which such organisations had been set up, a task that, as he put, involved "little more than taking a picture". The foundation of Bikers for Britain, for example, involved going to a motorbike event and asking a small group of attendees to pose for a photograph. Our source said the bikers in the picture were never asked for their views on the European Union and that, ironically, a good number of them were EU migrants. While Bikers for Britain was not mentioned in the designation application, the nature of its foundation demonstrates that even "grassroots" Vote Leave affiliates were the product of a top-down organisation.

Perhaps Vote Leave's most audacious claim came when the application described "talking to leaders of other potential applicants for designation, to discuss how our activities might be coordinated. There have been at least six attempts to explore how Leave.EU/GO/UKIP could work more closely and avoid duplication of resources. Unfortunately despite a constant willingness by Vote Leave to try to bridge the major strategic gaps, nothing constructive has come of this." Given Vote Leave's calculation of the fatal cost of involving UKIP, and the tight grip they sought to keep on the Leave campaign, such claims infuriated those who had spent nearly a year trying to find a way for the Leave coalition to work together.

The GO Movement's competing pitch also pointed to a long list of Leave groups that supported it. As well as Grassroots Out and Leave.EU, there were independent organisations such as the Bow Group, a conservative think tank; the People's Pledge and the Democracy Movement, both Eurosceptic campaigns; GO spinoffs like Conservatives GO, Liberals GO, Health Professionals GO, LBGT GO, Wales GO, Steel GO, Teachers GO and, surely the most obscure of them all given that there would be just 800 Leave voters there, Gibraltar GO.

GO described their plan to go further than just an "SW1 'air war'"; the referendum, they argued, "has to be fought street by street, door by door, elector by elector, vote by vote". They claimed that "there is no political, geographic, demographic, social or regional group our organisation doesn't touch."

The Electoral Commission's job was to designate official status to whichever "appears to us to represent those campaigning for that outcome to the greatest extent" and, on 13 April, it was announced that Vote Leave had won the contest.

The scoring system used by the commission revealed how close Banks's team had come to causing a major upset: Vote Leave 49, the GO Movement 45. The Commission's decision came down to its finding that, though both campaigns "demonstrate support from a wide range of groups representing different interests", "'Vote Leave Ltd' better demonstrated the depth of representation in their support from those campaigning at a regional and local level" and "provided well-developed plans and structures for how they would support other campaigning organisations. Their offer of support is not conditional on organisations agreeing to deliver messages or activity on their behalf and there is an established forum with the specific intended purpose of allowing an exchange of views between campaigners. By contrast the approach from 'GO Movement Ltd' is based on other campaigners signing formalised agreements as 'affiliates'."

Arron Banks did not take the news well. In a flurry of press releases fired off immediately after the decision he flirted with a legal challenge to the decision. Eventually, though, he said that, however strong his case might be, he would accept Vote Leave's official status because to do otherwise would gravely jeopardise the chances of a Leave vote in the referendum.

Even after their victory in the referendum, Leave.EU/GO-sympathising Leave campaigners remained bitter about designation, with phrases like "establishment stitch-up" being the preferred characterisation of the Electoral Commission's decision. "Bloody hell, does the establishment work in this country," was how Farage reflected on the decision after 23 June. Various conspiracy theories still surround the decision to designate Vote Leave, with UKIP activists making much of Vote Leave supporters claiming they knew they would win designation before the result had officially been announced. One claim that has been confirmed to us is that Vote Leave had an embarrassing and amateurish close shave with the designation application deadline, thanks to confusion over whether it was the end of the working day or midnight on 31 March. According to a Vote Leave board member, staff from the organisation arrived at the Electoral Commission offices, application in hand, only to find nobody there. Thankfully they eventually found a way to submit their paperwork in time. For an organisation with the backing of some of the most senior politicians in the country to have failed in its sole purpose of fighting the most important vote in a generation because of a deadline mix up would have been a new low for the already chaotic Leave side.

Just as Vote Leave figures thought that, with designation secured, they could breathe easily and concentrate on the short campaign ahead of them, unhappiness within their ranks boiled over. John Mills was one of the few veterans of the 1975 referendum involved in the 2016 vote. A large – in 2013, the largest individual, with a gift of shares worth over £1.6 million – donor to the Labour Party, he had grown used to being, if not the sole Labour figure in Eurosceptic circles, then one of the few from the party during his more than 40 years of campaigning on the issue. He had been an early donor to Business for Britain and an unerring presence in the Leave coalition in the year-long build-up to the vote, including as Chairman of Vote Leave. Yet in April, after what he characterised to us as "a whole series of difficulties with campaigning for the Labour vote" this central figure in the organisation walked out of Vote Leave altogether, instead focusing entirely on Labour Leave for the remainder of the campaign. Mills disagreed with the way the campaign was being run, and relations "in particular with Dominic Cummings" suffered as a result. Above all, though, Mills left Vote Leave because Labour Leave campaigners – especially Kate Hoey and Brendan Chilton – were, according to Mills, made to feel so unwelcome at Vote Leave that they simply would not go to its Victoria Embankment offices. "This was partly because Vote Leave was a rather Conservative organisation," said Mills, but also because of personality clashes, "largely to do with Cummings". Mills says of Cummings that he found him "very sharp, very bright" but, he added, "I don't think I am breaking new ground in saying he does have deficiencies."

***

In a short film made for the BBC after the referendum, Matthew Elliott said that one of his challenges during the campaign was "fighting UKIP". It may have struck viewers as odd that the man behind the official campaign to take the UK out of the EU saw UKIP, the only political party committed to leaving the EU, as somehow not on his side. While in-fighting and personality clashes were nothing new for hardened Eurosceptics, they were dismayed that so much of the year that separated the general election and the referendum was spent worrying about Leave disunity. Numerous senior Leave donors and campaigners related to us their frustration that, however hard they tried, attempts to foster at least a basic level of cooperation between various Brexit factions came to nothing.

The impasse can in part be explained by the colossal personality clash between, on the one hand, Elliott and Cummings, and on the other, Arron Banks. That clash did not end with the designation decision. In May, Banks sent the mobile numbers of Elliott, Cummings, Carswell and others to his supporters, urging them to pressure the "backstairs crawlers behind the creaking Vote Leave operation" to include Farage in the BBC's Wembley Arena debate. But behind the "slagging match" was a more substantive difference of opinion about what the Leave campaign should look like. Given the colourful spats, it was no surprise that stories of Leave ferrets in a bag, squandering the referendum they called for, became such a dominant theme of the campaign. The designation race certainly meant the Leave camp did not project the image of competency and trustworthiness that would have appealed to undecided voters. And the uncertainty over who would win official status meant some Leave backers were reluctant to donate money before the April decision, meaning Vote Leave did not raise as much early on as it had expected.

Yet despite the tremendous amount of bad blood between the camps, and as counterintuitive as it sounds, the divisions that exasperated so many on the Leave side in the end worked to their advantage. The pressure being applied on Vote Leave by Leave.EU – and the threat of humiliation if they did not win designation – focused Vote Leave minds early on. If competition meant sleepless nights for Elliott and Cummings, it also meant a better Leave campaign. Over at Leave.EU, Banks's determination to beat Vote Leave meant he spent heavily on the campaign in late 2015 and early 2016. Looking back on the designation saga, Peter Bone said: "As it turned out, it was a huge benefit, because ten times more work was done with all of us trying to impress the Electoral Commission. If we'd united under one umbrella I don't think one tenth of the work would have been done during that period. As with all competitions it makes you do things better. Nobody set out to do that but it was a by-product of what happened."

While division was an accidental boon to the Leave campaign early on by forcing Brexiteers to double their efforts, as the referendum approached it created important distance between the distinctive Leave tribes. Coming together as a unified campaign would not have meant an end to the differences of opinion and personalities. Indeed, with the need to reach agreement on countless campaign decisions, it would certainly have led to even uglier altercations. Is it likely that a campaign as ideologically diverse and involving as many egos would have the agility and ruthlessness needed to fight a difficult national campaign? And if there were any doubts as to how difficult the task ahead of them would be, they would quickly disappear when the government machine's Remain campaign sprang into action.

George Osborne, alongside Liz Truss, introduces the Treasury's report on the economic impact of Brexit. Its warning that households would be £4,300 worse off if the UK left the EU was intended to be a pillar of Project Fear.

Matt Cardy/PA Wire/Press Association Images

Chapter Six:
Numbers Games

"Project Fear" began life as a joke in the offices of the Scottish Referendum's No campaign. According to Rob Shorthouse, the campaign's director of communications who coined the now ubiquitous phrase, it "was all about poking fun at the Nats [Scottish Nationalists] and their constant dismissal of every legitimate point raised by anyone and everyone as scaremongering". But an inside joke soon became a powerful political concept. After Scotland voted "No", it quickly became received wisdom that it was Project Fear that won it for the Unionists. The lesson, then, was that the way to win referendums was to heap nightmarish forecasts onto the electorate and scare them into voting for the status quo.

If you broadly define Project Fear as a political campaign highlighting the risks of the unknown, it was always going to make up a substantial part of the Remain side's defence of EU membership. There was little love lost between Brussels and the British electorate, for decades fed a steady diet of Euroscepticism by the press, so Remain had little option but to make a pragmatic lesser-of-two-evils economic case to the country.

Andrew (Lord) Cooper, the pollster and close friend of the Prime Minister who provided the polling for the Remain campaign, broke the electorate down into seven segments. There were the two groups more or less beyond the reach of Stronger In: "strong sceptics" and "EU hostiles". At the other end of the spectrum were the "ardent internationalists", "comfortable Europhiles" and "engaged metropolitans" whose votes the Prime Minister could count on. In between were two crucial groups: "disengaged middle" and "head v. heart". Cooper's slicing and dicing was really only a restatement of what everyone already knew: that the middle chunk of the electorate, Eurosceptic but risk-averse and sensitive to the economic consequences of any political decision, would play a decisive role on 23 June.

It was these voters Project Fear was targeted at and so it was these voters that George Osborne hoped were listening when he spoke at the National Composite Centre in Bath on 18 April. The venue, where British scientists work at the cutting edge of carbon fibre technology, housed just the sort of dynamic hyper-modern activity politicians are keen to associate themselves with when talking about the economy. Osborne, flanked by his cabinet colleagues Liz Truss, Stephen Crabb and Amber Rudd, was there to present to the country the findings of the Treasury's analysis of the long-term economic effects of Brexit. Even committed Remain supporters conceded that the report was only ever intended as a weapon to be used by the Chancellor during the referendum campaign. That back-to-front starting point explained why a report that ran to more than 200 pages ended with one simple conclusion, a conclusion Osborne wanted to be heard loud and clear and which, in case voters somehow missed it, hung behind the Chancellor and his colleagues on large blue posters: "£4,300 a year. Cost to UK families if Britain leaves the EU."

Making the most of the credibility that comes with the backing of Treasury economists, Osborne said: "What many people are saying at the moment is that they don't have enough facts and information to make an informed decision." The Chancellor claimed that the Treasury's analysis "steps away from the rhetoric and set out the facts", and that those facts showed that "Britain will be permanently poorer if it left the European Union. Under any alternative we'd be poorer by £4,300 per household."

The starkness of the report's headline finding certainly meant the Chancellor's message had the potential to cut through to the "head v. heart" voters he so badly needed. The problem for Osborne and his Remain colleagues was that to get to the number they hoped would be effective, they had used eccentric and at times dishonest methodology. Even those otherwise sympathetic to Osborne's side of the argument were troubled by the precedent set by the Treasury report. Spectator editor Fraser Nelson typified the response to the Treasury report when he described George Osborne's "dishonesty" as "breathtaking": "For anyone who cares about honesty in politics and the abuse (and reporting) of statistics, this is an interesting case study." Firstly, there was Osborne's linguistic sleight of hand when it came to his use of the word "poorer". When the Chancellor said households would be £4,300 poorer outside the EU, voters could be forgiven for missing that what the Treasury report in fact claimed was that if the UK left the EU, the economy would have grown by just under 30 per cent by 2030 rather than by 37 per cent if we chose to remain. In other words, whether or not we left the EU, the British economy would expand by around a third over the next decade and a half.

Osborne's manipulations went further: to arrive at a soundbite that he thought most likely to get through to voters – an amount per household – the Treasury report simply divided GDP by the number of UK households. So Osborne was talking about GDP per household (not a measurement used anywhere else), not household income. And his projections did not factor in any change in the number of households. Why? Because if he had done so, the likelihood that immigration levels would be higher if the UK remained a member of the EU would have shrunk the headline number.

Osborne had claimed to give voters the facts; instead, he had served up politically-driven economic projections and then presented them in the most flattering light possible. The problems with the report were widely discussed and what could have been a credible and highly persuasive boost for Remain was significantly undermined because, not for the first time in his career, the Chancellor prioritised political advantage to the exclusion of economic integrity. The warning was also too specific. While the case for continued EU membership was built on the dangerous uncertainty that would come with a Leave vote, Treasury economists claimed to know what the impact of leaving would be on household income a decade and a half in the future. The mixed messages neutralised one another, with the sense that a future outside the EU was uncertain undermining the plausibility of the Treasury report and the Treasury report inadvertently capping the relative cost of Brexit at £4,300.

If the Treasury report had not landed in the way many Remain campaigners had hoped, they were still confident Project Fear would gain traction later in April, when the government unveiled what it thought was the ideal cheerleader for its cause. In the final year of his Presidency, Barack Obama was held in high esteem by the British. Downing Street's logical calculation was that words of warning coming from the US President would be listened to especially intently by British voters. On a visit to London, the President, speaking at a joint press conference with David Cameron, told Britain: "I think [the EU] helps your economy," adding: "Precisely because we're bound at the hip I want you to know that." Obama's words of advice came with the caveat that "this is a decision for the people of the United Kingdom to make. I'm not coming here to fix any votes. I'm not casting a vote myself. I am offering my opinion, and in democracies everybody should want more information, not less, and you shouldn't be afraid to hear an argument being made." Four more words uttered by the President would make headlines: "back of the queue".

Obama warned that if the UK left the EU, an Anglo-American trade deal would be low on the UK's closest ally's list of priorities.

Despite Obama's caveats about the referendum decision being one for the British people, his comment hit a nerve. The Leave side successfully hammed up their outrage at an American President "coming over here and telling us how to vote", characterising his intervention as bullying rather than the friendly advice Downing Street had hoped it would be received as. They also pointed out that Obama would not be President when the time came to negotiate a trade deal, so his views were not necessarily worth placing too much weight on. Conspiratorially-inclined Brexiteers pointed to the President's use of the word "queue", instead of the more American "line", as evidence that the phrase had been fed to him by Downing Street, while Boris Johnson responded distastefully, if not altogether ineffectively, in the *Telegraph* when he wrote that the "part-Kenyan" President had an "ancestral dislike of the British Empire". The electorate's response to the presidential visit, visible in the polls as an "Obama bounce" for Leave, was an encouraging sign for the Brexiteers. In Lord Owen's view, Obama's intervention boosted the Leave side by three to five per cent. If the British people were willing to ignore Obama's words of advice, perhaps Remain's words of warning in general were falling on deaf ears.

Early in the campaign, Project Fear was potent not because of one knock-out economic claim – Osborne had tried, and failed, to deliver that with the Treasury report and Obama's intervention had backfired – but because it was so unremitting. A week before the publication of Osborne's report, the government spent more than £9 million on a leaflet sent to every UK household setting out the "key facts" that explained why "we are stronger, safer and better off in the EU". Given that the spending limit for Vote Leave was £7 million, Leavers were apoplectic at the move. Peter Bone summed up his side's reaction when he called the leaflet "immoral, undemocratic and against what the government had promised". The sending out of the leaflet was particularly galling to Leavers as a similar thing had happened during the 1975 referendum campaign. Then every household received three leaflets, one from each of the campaigns and one from the government also making the case from remaining in the EEC. Bone says that Tory pro-Leave MPs had pressed the government in private during the parliamentary debates on the Referendum bill on whether a similar gambit was planned for this time – and were categorically assured that it was not.

Backing up the government line was almost a full house of economic heavyweights. Bank of England Governor Mark Carney issued several warnings of the economic damage he thought a Leave vote would wreak. In May he said Brexit "could lead to a materially lower path for growth and a materially higher path for inflation". Christine Lagarde, managing director of the International Monetary Fund, echoed the Governor's warning when she said: "We have done our homework and we haven't found anything positive to say about a Brexit vote."

Leave campaigners tend not to have fond memories of the early stages of the campaign. One described to us being hit in April and May by "wave after wave" of arguments against leaving the EU, crafted with the help of Whitehall and benefitting from the added credibility of being official government policy. But on 27 May, all that ended.

Purdah, according to the Cabinet Manual, means "the deferral of activity such as: taking or announcing major policy decisions; entering into large/contentious procurement contracts or significant long-term commitments; and making some senior public appointments and approving senior civil service appointments, provided that such postponement would not be detrimental to the national interest or wasteful of public money". It kicks in 28 days before a general election and is an essential ingredient for a fair contest between the governing party and the opposition. Arguably the most important battle fought by Brexiteers against Project Fear took place in September 2015, when the Referendum bill was making its way through Parliament. One of the questions was whether or not purdah of the sort that applies to general elections should be in force for the referendum. Cameron, with the help of Cabinet Secretary Jeremy Haywood, sought to avoid the application of purdah to the referendum, arguing that it would make government "unworkable" during the referendum period. Leavers argued that a fair fight would be impossible without it. Had the Prime Minister got his way, it is hard to believe the government machine would have been doing anything other than making the case for a Remain vote in those all-important final 28 days. That it was unable to do so was thanks not only to the 37 Conservatives who rebelled on the purdah question, but also to Labour and the SNP who took the opportunity to humiliate the government with a Commons defeat of 312 votes to 285. In hindsight,

Labour and SNP MPs, the overwhelming majority of whom backed EU membership, must regret their prioritisation of short-term political point-scoring over giving their side of the referendum the best possible chances of victory. Leavers look back on this early skirmish in the Commons as a pivotal moment. Bernard Jenkin saw purdah as a "decisive" factor in the referendum. "Look how the atmosphere changed overnight," he said of the moment purdah kicked in. "Suddenly the media operation at Vote Leave started getting positive coverage."

It was during these battles that the Brexiteers also ensured that the version of the electoral roll used for general elections and for the 2011 AV referendum would be used for the forthcoming vote. The government had initially favoured applying the version of the electoral roll that is used for European and local elections for the referendum, which also allows citizens of EU member countries resident in the UK to vote. It can safely be assumed that these EU citizens, if they did turn out to vote, would break overwhelmingly to Remain.

Of course, purdah did not mean an end to Project Fear. Throughout the final 28 days Cameron and his Remain colleagues reiterated the conclusions of government reports designed to put the electorate off voting Leave. As well as being warned of the impact of Brexit on household incomes, voters were told that wages would fall, unemployment would rise, house prices would be hit and holidays would become more expensive. But in the final weeks of the campaign, with some polls showing Leave in the lead, the Brexiteers themselves believed and dreaded that the Remain camp would take Project Fear to an even greater level of intensity.

That final barrage came from George Osborne, already the architect of one ineffective economic intervention in the referendum. With less than two weeks to go to polling day, the Chancellor was looking for a way to make the point that a vote for Brexit would be a vote for economic hardship. To do so, he told voters what he would have to do as Chancellor if Leave won. Brexit, he said, would create a £30 billion hole in the public finances. He and his predecessor and fellow Remain campaigner Alistair Darling together published a list of the sort of measures that would have to be implemented. It included a 2p rise in the basic rate of income tax to 22 per cent, a 3p rise in the higher rate to 43 per cent and a five per cent rise in inheritance tax to 45 per cent. Alcohol and petrol duties would increase by five per cent. Spending cuts, including a two per cent cut for health, defence and education, would come to £15 billion. Not only did the authority of Osborne's announcement quickly unravel, with 57 Conservative MPs putting their name to a letter saying they would refuse to back such a proposal, but it also came to be seen by voters as an act of political sadism. With its melodramatic economic assumptions and a negative, even threatening tone that turned voters off, the punishment budget, as it came to be known, typified all the tactical failings of Project Fear.

After the result, many commentators characterised the referendum as a contest between competing priorities: Remain may have won the economic argument, but Leave won the immigration debate, and the latter trumped the former. Implicit in this characterisation of the campaign is a conclusion that the vote to Leave was an act of knowing economic self-destruction. Voters, according to this argument, either had nothing to lose from Brexit or were so concerned about immigration that they simply didn't care if leaving the EU made them poorer. This conclusion fails to grasp the nature of the Leave vote. There is no reason to believe thinking changed significantly from John Curtice's January 2016 report, based on a face-to-face survey of 3,000 voters, about the nature of their views on the EU. Of those who thought the economy would be worse-off if the UK left the EU, a paltry six per cent supported withdrawal anyway. Whatever the relative ranking of immigration versus economics by voters, the presumption that Remain won the economic argument is mistaken. In polls conducted during the final stages of the campaign, when voters were asked whether they thought leaving the EU would make the UK either worse-off, better-off or neither richer nor poorer, the largest group were those that thought Brexit would make us worse-off. But the groups that thought either that Brexit would make the UK richer or would not make a difference were not far behind. In other words, a majority of voters saw no economic harm in Brexit.

Such an outcome is nothing more than a resounding failure for Project Fear. While those in favour of Brexit saw a strong economic case for leaving what they thought was a customs union shrinking in relative economic size and run by a cumbersome, outdated organisation with anti-business instincts in its DNA, most had enough self-awareness to realise that, in conventional electoral terms, the economic case for Leave was not readily appealing. First, it involved a substantial amount of uncertainty.

Second, it relied on principles rather than specific promises and forecasts. Third, many Leavers admitted (though, as the vote approached, generally not in public) that Brexit would trade short-term stability for long-term prosperity. Given this difficult sell, the Leave campaign's goal was "to fight Project Fear to a standstill", as an early Business for Britain operative put it to us.

How did the Leave campaign pull off such a feat? Why did voters reach different economic conclusions to the Treasury, the Bank of England, the major investment banks and practically every big multinational corporation? It does appear that the early work done by Business for Britain did help to at least muddy the electorate's sense of what business thought of EU membership, drawing important distinctions between large corporations and entrepreneurs and small businesses. Vote Leave's aggressive rebuttal of the economic arguments against Brexit also paid off. The relentlessness with which Leave campaigners accused their opponents of lacking credibility, being in the pocket of the EU, or in some other way having a vested interest in a Remain vote neutralised numerous economic arguments against Brexit, however valid they may have been. But cunningly drafted press releases do not come close to explaining such an unprecedented dismissal of economic authority figures.

The broader political climate in which the referendum took place was undoubtedly a contributory factor. That the referendum came several years into the protracted and multi-phase eurozone crisis, with no end in sight to the economic pain being felt by Mediterranean member states stuck with debts they will probably never pay off and unemployment rates that remain stubbornly high, meant that rather than believe tendentious forecasts of the economic doom and gloom that would engulf the UK if they voted Leave, voters had, across the Channel, a more visceral illustration of what the EU had come to stand for economically.

More generally, thanks in part to the long shadow cast by the financial crisis, the vote came at a time when respect for the views of traditionally credible institutions and individuals was at an all-time low. A YouGov poll conducted two weeks before polling day which asked voters "Thinking of the referendum, how much do you trust the following types of people?", suggested that the erosion of faith in authority figures went further than economics.

	Trust	Don't trust
People from well-known businesses	37	43
People from well-known charities	37	40
Think tanks (e.g. the IFS)	28	44
Economists	38	39
People from international organisations (like the UN and IMF)	32	46
People from the Bank of England	36	45
Political leaders of other countries	14	67
Politicians from Britain	13	72
Academics	43	37
Newspaper journalists	10	74
Well-known sportspeople	10	64
Well-known actors and entertainers	12	61
Senior religious figures	15	61

The results confirmed what Michael Gove said more concisely during a Sky News town hall interview in the final stages of the campaign: "This country has had enough of experts." In such a climate is it surprising that a campaign built around trusting the experts did not work?

However difficult the environment they were operating in, much of the blame still lies with the Remain campaign. When Bernard Jenkin, a Vote Leave director, heard that Project Fear of the sort implemented in Scotland would be used in the referendum, he says he "jumped for joy". Downing Street's analysis of the Scottish vote seems to have gone no deeper than assuming the winning side's strategy must have worked. Such an analysis ignores the fact that while the Unionist side won the referendum, public opinion moved towards independence during the campaign. In other words, while Project Fear was in full swing, Scots became keener on leaving the Union than they had been before. Virtually no polls have ever given Scottish independence a lead, except for two conducted in the midst of Unionist doomsaying.

The Remain camp's analysis of the 2014 vote also lacked a proper appreciation of the ways in which the European question differed from Scottish independence. In 2014, Alex Salmond presented a fully fleshed-out fiscal plan for an independent Scotland, underpinned by the high price of oil, something which Unionists could poke holes in. Leave campaigners, by contrast, always planned to keep their arguments vague, avoiding a detailed exit plan to avoid such scrutiny. One campaigner involved in Business for Britain and then Vote Leave explained to us that it was decided "very early on not to have an exit plan". He explained: "It doesn't matter what your plan is, you immediately make yourself a hostage to fortune." The downside for Leave, as became clear, was "you risk the other side saying that you don't have a plan, to which you say 'Well, we're not the government'." If you play it right, "you bring the man in who wants the Norway option, the man who wants whatever option and so on, and then say 'look, there's a whole range of options, and if you like any of them, join our coalition'." As well as presenting a plan for Remain to pick apart, opting for a preferred plan would have meant "inviting your own side to split".

It is also worth remembering that much of the economic debate in the Scottish referendum was not focused on unconvincingly specific forecasts about the consequences of upsetting the status quo, as with, for example, the Treasury's report ahead of the EU vote. Instead it was a question of control: if Scots were uneasy about their future as an independent state, it was because nationalists failed to convince voters that Scotland would be in command of its own destiny. Perhaps then, the lesson from Project Fear was that the idea of control had electoral potency. At least one side of the EU referendum battle was paying attention.

***

If Remain's Project Fear involved the dubious use of statistics and forecasts, the Leave side played numbers games of their own. Of all the questionable claims made by both sides of the referendum campaign, none attracted more attention than the message emblazoned on the side of the Vote Leave battle bus that took Boris Johnson, Michael Gove and other Brexiteers around the country: "We send the EU £350 million. Let's fund our NHS instead". The claim also played a starring role in Vote Leave leaflets and broadcasts; it was the single most repeated assertion made by the campaign.

The figure of £350 million was derived by taking the UK's gross contribution to the EU in 2014, £18,777 million, and dividing it by 52, resulting in £361 million, which was then rounded down for neatness. The figure takes no account of the £4.4 billion rebate negotiated by Margaret

Thatcher and in place since 1985, which is deducted at source (i.e. never sent to Brussels). In 2014 the UK received back nearly £4.5 billion in various EU grants, the vast bulk for agricultural support and regional development aid, much of which will continue – paid for by British taxpayers – after the UK leaves the EU. The figure of £350 million is, at best, debatable. What cannot be argued with is there will not be £350 million which can simply be given to the NHS on leaving the EU.

The use of the figure was extremely controversial with many of Vote Leave supporters. It prompted Ruth Lea to resign from the campaign, making the case for Brexit independently. Farage believes it was a big mistake. He described it to us as "dreadful, absolutely ill-thought-out" and something "our side is still being pilloried for and will be for the next 20 years", though perhaps this verdict is not surprising given his rivalry with the official campaign. But politicians who took part in Vote Leave's regular Thursday campaign meeting were also unhappy with the number. When asked about it, one very senior politician replied, "Well, I never went on the bus. Draw your own conclusions." Another at the very top of the campaign said, "I can still put together an argument to justify its use." Hardly a ringing endorsement.

We have spoken to most of Vote Leave's largest donors and we could find only one who was happy with £350 million. Many felt the figure was dishonest and reduced their noble cause to the same level as Project Fear. And the message of giving the money to the NHS did not sit well with donors who believed in reducing the size of the state and in reforming public services.

Why was the figure used? One explanation, put to us by a director of Vote Leave, is that it was simply shoddy research – the campaign had a very small and inexperienced research team and it came up with the wrong figure. Cummings and Elliott started to use the figure for their literature and were too proud to back down. When challenged about the figure the response would come, "That train has left the station."

Another explanation – unsurprisingly preferred by Elliott and Cummings – is that the figure was deliberately picked by them because it was defendable but less than robust. By chucking a dodgy number into the mix, the figure was endlessly debated. It would lead news items – and be repeated ad nauseam. The figure would stick in the public's minds. The Remainers would have to come out with their own figure, which would also sound very large to voters. Saying we send only £190 million per week to Brussels is not the ideal starting point if you are defending the UK's EU membership.

Elliott had pulled off the same trick in 2011 when he ran the successful No to AV campaign. He attached a rather dubious figure to the cost of changing the electoral system and asked voters if they wouldn't rather spend the money on nurses. The figure was challenged and debated. Even though extremely trivial in terms of government expenditure, it stuck in people's minds.

Whether a cock-up or a stroke of genius, £350 million certainly worked on the ground. Campaigners have told us it was frequently repeated back to them on the doorstep and at street stalls, unprompted. One Vote Leave insider told us he found the use of £350 million, and its effectiveness, deeply unsettling. The message, he said, is that in politics it pays to lie.

At the halfway stage of the designated campaign period, very few foresaw the counterintuitive outcomes to the numbers games being played by both sides – that Project Fear would be met by a shrug from the electorate, and that settling on a number your opposition could comfortably pick apart would work to your advantage. Many Leave campaigners worried that the pre-purdah government blitzkrieg would win round enough undecided voters and soft Eurosceptics to put a Leave vote out of reach. Their concern was not just that the response to Project Fear was inadequate; they were also frustrated by the prominence of the figure of £350 million, a number they had already grown tired of defending, and unhappy with the use of "take control", Vote Leave's Cummings-inspired slogan. Malcolm Pearson, in a memo disseminated widely throughout the Leave moment, took measure of what he saw to be the Leave side's problems. The blame, as he saw it, lay with the official campaign:

> . . . there is increasing anxiety among many senior people on the Leave side that the Vote Leave campaign, masterminded by Cummings and Elliott, is failing. These leading supporters include major funders, senior Tory and Labour politicians, together with other leading campaigners and economists.
>
> Outside Vote Leave itself, no one is saying, or writing, that it is a well-run campaign with a clear strategy.
>
> The campaign strategy promoted by Cummings and Elliott was

centred around the economic case, with an unwillingness to seriously address immigration; only very belatedly is this being talked about. The campaign slogan of "take control", designed by Elliott and Cummings, is meaningless compared to the effective Remain slogan of "Safer, stronger and better off In" which they repeat with relentless discipline.

He went on to criticise Vote Leave's handling of the air war, focused on £350 million going to the NHS, which he called "the wrong number on the wrong thing", and the ground war, in which he said there were "far too few" posters, banners and other resources leading to "huge frustration/depression amongst ground campaigners". He said Vote Leave leaflets were so poor "many [volunteers] refuse even to hand them out. Many ground troops are becoming demoralised to the point that they may begin to give up, fearing that we have lost." Pearson characterised the Leave campaign as "a depressing blue on blue male ego battle, between Boris and Dave, with a splash of Michael, which is turning off Tory voters and leaving the rest more than cold . . . The polls are now turning against us and the markets think it is all over." Pearson ended his memo thus: "The key thrust of Dominic and Matthew's business plan is not working. Can your top team truly change their approach, or is another solution needed?"

With less than a month to go, the Leave coalition was no less awkward, the factions no more comfortable with one another's roles in the referendum debate and no closer to working together than they had been before designation. When Pearson complained of Vote Leave's "unwillingness" to discuss immigration, he was bringing up not only the biggest ideological fissure in the Brexit camp but the issue that would, for better or for worse, come to dominate the final stages of the campaign. ⸙

Nigel Farage unveils his party's now infamous Breaking Point poster. According to one UKIP campaigner, they had more provocative posters planned.

Philip Toscano/PA Wire/Press Association Images

Chapter Seven:
Breaking Point

On 26 May, less than a month before the referendum, the Office for National Statistics (ONS) delivered some unwelcome news for Cameron and the Remain campaign: in 2015 net long-term migration to the UK – the difference between the number of people coming to live in the UK and the number leaving – had reached 333,000, its highest-ever level for a calendar year and only 3,000 below its highest level for any 12-month period. In the run-up to the 2010 general election Cameron had stated: "We would like to see net immigration in the tens of thousand, rather than hundreds of thousand." This was repeated as a promise in the Conservative manifesto that year and the coalition government had stated its intention of meeting this target by 2015. Yet, largely thanks to the UK's recovery from recession, migration levels have risen sharply since then. In 2009 net migration stood at 196,000; the annual numbers were now more than 68 per cent higher than they were when Cameron made his pledge.

For most of the 1990s, annual net migration to the UK had been in the "tens of thousands", rising rapidly only towards the end of the decade. Indeed, in 1992 and 1993 the UK had experienced very modest net emigration of 13,000 and 1,000 respectively. By 1999, net migration hit 163,000 per year. Even in the 1990s, levels of net migration were high by historical standards. Between 1961 and 1981 the UK experienced net emigration, averaging 20,000 per year, and in the 1980s net immigration stood, on average, in the thousands.

Turning to the absolute numbers, the levels of immigration the UK is experiencing today are also totally unprecedented. In 1961, the height of primary migration to the UK from the Commonwealth, 136,400 people arrived to settle in the UK. This prompted the first minor restrictions on Commonwealth immigration to be imposed in 1962 with much stricter restrictions following in 1968. Up to that point, immigration from the Commonwealth was pretty much unrestricted and its then population of more than 800 million had the right to settle in the UK. Of course, the vast majority of this population was too poor at that time to contemplate the journey to Britain. In 2015, according to ONS figures, 630,000 people settled in the UK, more than four and a half times the 1961 figure. Today's levels of immigration are at a completely different level from those that prompted Enoch Powell's infamous "Rivers of Blood" speech in 1968 or the rise of the National Front in the 1970s.

A significant part of this rise, although never a majority, is accounted for by migration from the eight Central and Eastern European states which joined the EU in 2004, especially Poland as with its 38 million people it has by far the largest population of the eight, and then later from Bulgaria and Romania, which joined in 2007. Citizens from these accession states enjoyed the rights of free movement from the moment their countries joined the EU; existing members were entitled to impose restrictions on the right to work on people from the new member countries for a period of seven years. The Blair government, however, chose not to do so in regard to the 2004 members, but did do so for Bulgaria and Romania. These restrictions expired in January 2014. The timing enabled UKIP to make an issue out of a new tranche of expected Bulgarian and Romanian migrants, especially from those countries' large Roma communities, arriving in the run-up to that year's European elections.

In 2015 according to ONS figures, net migration from EU citizens to the UK stood at 184,000, up 10,000 from 2014: 270,000 non-UK EU citizens moved to the UK and 86,000 left. Some 630,000 – a substantially larger number – new National Insurance (NI) numbers, needed by all those who legally work in the UK, were issued to EU nationals in the year to March 2016. This has led some to doubt about the accuracy of the ONS migration numbers, which are estimates based on the International Passenger Survey – interviews conducted at airports, ports, and train and coach terminals. Some of the explanation for the discrepancy is that the migration figures do not include people who come to work in the UK for less than a year; they are not classed as long-term migrants. It is also true that some arrivals from previous years have only started working more recently, so only now require NI numbers. Nevertheless, the discrepancy – much more than twice as many NI numbers issued than the number of people coming to settle in the UK – is not easily explained away.

Of course, not all EU nationals coming to the UK are from the new member states. The eurozone crisis has brought many southern Europeans to the UK in search of work, and at the wealthier end of the spectrum there is no shortage of Dutch, French, German and Italian bankers working in London. ONS estimates suggest that 48 per cent of 2015 EU migrants came from the old EU, 26 per cent from the 2004 Central and East European accession states, and 25 per cent from Bulgaria and Romania. Of the new NI numbers issued in the year to March 2016, 228,000 were to citizens of the old EU, 180,000 to the 2004 EU Eight and 219,000 to Bulgarians and Romanians. The last two countries' 27 million people – Romania with nearly 20 million is much the larger – represent 3.5 per cent of the EU's total population but received 35 per cent of the new NI numbers.

Cameron believed that the British public's single biggest issue with the EU was free movement – and by the tests he himself had set, his government was failing. The high levels of migration to the UK, that so many people wanted to move here, could be celebrated as a sign of Britain's success – but that was not an argument many politicians were willing to make. Immigration had become a significant concern for the electorate. The problem politicians have had with debating it is that the subject had been made so toxic so long ago by the actions of Enoch Powell – and, yes, the "Rivers of Blood" speech, whatever the merits of an educated, civilised man with intelligent views on other issues, is every bit as poisonous as it has been deemed to be by the Left – and then by the far Right in the 1970s. The fact that racists had banged on about immigration when it was actually at fairly low levels meant that it was extremely difficult for legitimate concerns to be raised when immigration was running at extremely high levels.

A retired diplomat, Sir Andrew – now Lord – Green, who had served as ambassador to Syria and Saudi Arabia, and an Oxford University professor of demography, David Coleman, believed it was vital to make public discussion of the costs of large-scale immigration socially acceptable again. In pursuit of this aim they established Migration Watch in 2001. It was a surprise to many that two such respectable establishment figures as Green and Coleman were willing to make the case for much tighter immigration controls. The way Migration Watch made its case – with calm, measured arguments about the pressure on schooling and healthcare, the impact on low-skilled wages, the increased demand for housing – gradually made it more acceptable for mainstream politicians to say that migrant numbers had to come down.

There are persuasive economic arguments to be made in favour of large-scale migration, but these have little resonance with most of the electorate. Perhaps the best example of this disconnect was the remarkably inept comments of the chairman of the Remain campaign, Stuart Rose. In March 2016 he stated that leaving the EU would drive up wages for low-skilled work and would thus be very bad for the economy. Whatever the economic merits of Lord Rose's argument, it was certainly no way to win a referendum, and explains why little more of him was seen during the referendum campaign.

The problem for Leave campaigners was how to handle immigration. It was the single most important issue for large sections of the electorate but the legacy of how immigration had been discussed by some in the past meant that, if it was not extremely carefully handled, it would turn Brexit toxic for other voters. Leave.EU, Farage and those around him took the view that the way to win the referendum was by indelibly linking in the electorate's mind large-scale immigration with membership of the EU. Doing so would encourage people who did not usually vote, and in some cases had never voted, to come out and vote in the referendum – and win it for Leave. Elliott and Vote Leave argued that the wrong kind of messaging on immigration would be so off-putting to swing voters that they would be pushed to vote for Remain, and the referendum would be lost. As one of the campaigners involved in Vote Leave from day one told us, "We were very nervous about immigration. We didn't want to do it."

In the immediate aftermath of the 2015 general election, soon after Farage had stepped down as leader of UKIP and then, just a few days later, been reinstated, Douglas Carswell described in *The Times* the way he thought the party should handle immigration:

> UKIP has been at its most persuasive when we have been most optimistic. Anger is never a great way to motivate people – at least not for very long. Instead of feeding the idea that EU membership is synonymous with immigration, UKIP should help draw attention to the myriad of ways in which being run by Brussels makes us worse off.

Farage described to us his reaction on reading this: "When Carswell wrote, we must not make immigration and EU membership synonymous, I thought, Christ, I've spent ten years trying to do just that." When we put to Farage the argument that an aggressive, unnuanced emphasis on immigration might have put off voters, his response was, "Oh yes, in Westminster, yeah. And Chelsea, God yeah. We could have turned off hundreds, literally hundreds. But in the rest of the country, perhaps, we would have attracted millions." Farage's opponents within his own party believe such a campaign would have been so toxic that it would have lost the referendum by a margin of 70 per cent to 30 per cent. The two wings of the Leave campaign – indeed the two wings of UKIP – had, in theory, wholly incompatible approaches as to how to deal with immigration as an issue.

To make the case for immigration being the central message of the Leave campaign, in December UKIP commissioned a private survey with a sample size of 10,000 – massive by the standards of the polling industry – to gauge how important the issue was to voters. The respondents were given a set of statements such as "Leaving would allow us to trade with the rest of the world" and "Leaving the EU will make us less exposed to Greece and other unstable economies and the risk we might have to bail them out", and asked to rank them in terms of their importance in deciding how to vote in the referendum.

The statement which had the highest resonance with those who had not yet decided how to vote or who would consider switching was "Leaving is the only way we can control our borders and set our own immigration policy." For 38 per cent of those in that category this was the single most important argument; the statement which came closest to it in terms of popularity was "Leaving would save the UK money which could be spent at home," getting the backing of only 18 per cent, followed by "Leaving is the only way that the UK can make its own laws and control its destiny," supported by 11.5 per cent. For 62 per cent of the same category of voter the immigration point came in the top three arguments.

Those opposed to the UKIP approach to the referendum argued that an emphasis on immigration might well appeal to those 4 million or so voters who had supported UKIP in the 2014 European elections or the 2015 general election, but these were in the bag already. What was needed, they would argue, was a message that appealed to swing voters. With their mega-poll, and in highlighting the responses of undecided voters, UKIP was trying to show that it was precisely a message on immigration that would appeal to the wavering portion of the electorate.

The UKIP argument is not as devastating a criticism of the Vote Leave stance as it might at first appear. The statement "Leaving is the only way we can control our borders and set our own immigration policy" in fact chimes perfectly with the one part of Cummings's strategy which – contrary to the reservations expressed by senior Leavers like Malcolm Pearson – was very smart, namely the use of "Vote Leave, Take Control" as the campaign's core message.

One can date the adoption of that slogan with some precision. Vote Leave was registered as a company on Friday, 18 September 2015, with two initial directors – Cummings and Elliott. Its name then, chosen and vigorously insisted upon by Cummings, in spite of the doubts expressed by his colleagues, was Vote Leave, Get Change Ltd. This name strongly suggests that Cummings still favoured a two-referendum strategy, i.e. if we vote to leave, we will have a better negotiating position, see what change we can get from the EU and, if necessary, put the new deal to a second referendum.

Something changed over that weekend. By Monday morning Cummings was insistent that the company's name needed to be changed immediately to just Vote Leave Ltd, and was asking why anyone had suggested as foolish a name as Vote Leave, Get Change. Vote Leave, Take Control was now the slogan that the campaign would be pushing.

Taking back control is an idea that people with very different ideologies can unite behind, for it says nothing about what will be done with that control. Kelvin Hopkins, the Labour MP for Luton North, is very much on the Labour Left and is a strong supporter of Jeremy Corbyn. He campaigned for Brexit, indeed has supported withdrawal for his entire political life, and was a regional agent for the campaign to leave the EEC in the 1975 referendum, because he believes that the EU is an inherently unreformable neoliberal and anti-socialist institution. Yet Hopkins explained he had no problems with working with Elliott, regardless of Elliott's pedigree as a neoliberal campaigner: "If you are campaigning for self-government, to take back control, that says nothing about what you will do with the control once you have it back."

Similarly, those respondents who strongly backed the assertion in the UKIP poll that "Leaving is the only way we can control our borders and set our own immigration policy" were not necessarily saying that they wanted a more restrictive immigration policy, merely that they wanted the UK to have democratic control over its immigration policy. In all likelihood, most of them did want a more restrictive immigration policy, but Cummings's Take Control message could appeal both to those who wanted to drastically reduce the numbers coming in and those who were not unduly worried about the numbers but wanted the decisions about immigration to be made in the UK. The charge of meaninglessness which had been levelled at the slogan by Lord Pearson was not wrong. Rather, the UKIP peer failed to see that meaninglessness was, in this case, useful.

After the ONS figures were published Vote Leave started to talk more explicitly about immigration in their campaign. Whether or not this was always the plan is disputed by people involved in drawing up the campaign's strategy. Some claim that the initial strategy – other than the Take Control message itself – was to avoid the issue of immigration entirely and that the campaign only started to talk about it out of a sense of panic. Others say that the plan all along was to move on to immigration later in the campaign once economic concerns had been addressed.

On 1 June Boris Johnson, flanked by Leave ministers Michael Gove and Priti Patel, outlined his support for an Australian-style points-based immigration policy. This had previously been adopted as UKIP policy in the run-up to the 2015 general election. The thinking behind the party's adoption of it was explained to us by a UKIP strategist. While the policy can be seen as fairer, for example, to Commonwealth professionals who want to come to the UK and is eminently respectable, what many voters hear is simply the message of limiting immigration. For many, when they hear Australian-style points-based system, what they are thinking is no – or extremely limited – immigration. In Farage's view, the adoption of this policy was when the referendum campaign turned around: "The day Boris and Gove did that was the day we started taking a lead in the polls."

The other issue closely linked to migration that Vote Leave adopted was Turkey's application to join the EU. Turkish membership of the EU alarmed many: a Muslim country with a population of 76 million and a GDP per capita on a par with that of Romania, one of the EU's two poorest members. Considering how many people had come to the UK from Romania, how many more might come over from the much larger Turkey? Vote Leave made the most of these concerns by providing on their website a map labelling only Turkey, Iraq and Syria. Playing on concern over the migrant crisis, their aim, clearly, was to make voters wonder how many more might come from those unstable countries.

The dishonesty in Vote Leave's line was the impression it gave that Turkish membership of the EU was imminent: indeed, it explicitly stated that Turkey could be a full member of the EU by 2020. Most informed commentators, however, thought it would be many years off, not least because it was very low on the agendas of France and Germany. Cameron had been a vocal supporter of Turkish membership, declaring in 2014 that "in terms of Turkish membership of the EU, I very much support that. That's a long-standing position of British foreign policy which I support." He had claimed to be the EU Prime Minister who was the biggest backer of Turkey's case. Yet now in response to Vote Leave's campaign Cameron claimed Turkish membership was not a realistic prospect – depending on when he was talking – for 30 years or until about the year 3000. What he was not willing to do – which he could easily have done – is say that he would have vetoed Turkish membership, something entirely within the powers of an EU member state's Prime Minister. This would not have entirely shut down the Turkey membership question – after all, Cameron's commitment would not bind future Prime Ministers – but it would have gone a long way towards it.

The irony of Vote Leave's Turkey campaign is that those at the heart of the organisation explained why a UKIP, Leave.EU-type approach centred on immigration would have been disastrous – and then when they themselves ran with immigration, they chose an innuendo-laden line that was far from clean. Vote Leave could have raised the type of untainted arguments that Migration Watch had focused on; they could have made the kind of points about the problems of mass migration that centre-left figures such as Lord Owen and Gisela Stuart made to us: the fact that in parts of the UK local schools and the NHS cannot cope with the extra demand on their services, the inability of the existing already overstretched infrastructure to cope, the downward pressure on wages and upward pressure on rents. Yet the campaign made none of these points and instead – let us be upfront about it – played up fears of hordes of brown-skinned Muslims descending on the UK.

There were very good reasons for Vote Leave not using the untarnished arguments against mass migration. By doing so they would clearly have tied themselves to a position of reducing migrant numbers, which they did not wish to do. With the Take Control slogan and support for an Australian-style points-based system, they were making no commitment on numbers and could appeal both to those who wanted a restrictive migration policy and those who wanted a permissive one. The Turkey line of attack entailed no direct policy implications and may have been extremely effective, but that does not mean that it was not deeply hypocritical, especially in the light of how it was done.

Electoral Commission rules meant that UKIP could spend up to £4 million on the referendum campaign – if they could raise that much. UKIP received £1.25 million in declarable donations, i.e. in donations of over £7,500, in the second quarter of 2016. Not all of these donations will have related to the referendum campaign – some will have been for the May 2016 London and Welsh elections – but there will also have been donations relating to the referendum received in other quarters. UKIP had a significant budget for the referendum fight, although significantly less than the full £4 million permitted. The party decided to spend the bulk of its money on a poster and newspaper advertising campaign during the last week of the referendum.

On 16 June – one week before the referendum – Farage unveiled UKIP's now infamous "Breaking Point" poster. It showed a line of migrants crossing the Croatia-Slovenia border at the height of the migrant crisis of 2015 with the words "Breaking Point" in large bold red lettering across it. The rest of the wording went: "The EU has failed us all. We must break free of the EU and take back control of our borders." UKIP had adopted Vote Leave's take back control message, yet this did nothing to make the poster go down any better with the official campaign. On seeing the poster there was real worry and consternation in Vote Leave's offices. There was a feeling that it would only damage the Leave vote.

When we asked Hannan about the poster he replied: "Just ask yourself, when you think about that Breaking Point poster, who was ever going to be impressed by it? Can you imagine any voter who was on the fence saying to himself, there is a refugee crisis in Europe, I'd better vote Leave now?" Why this argument, albeit perhaps to a slightly lesser extent, should not apply to Vote Leave's Turkey campaign is less clear.

Ninety minutes after the poster was launched in London, Jo Cox, the 41-year-old Labour MP for Batley and Spen in Yorkshire who had campaigned for Remain, was fatally shot in her constituency outside the library where she was about to hold her surgery. When Thomas Mair, the man charged with her murder, appeared at Westminster Magistrates Court he gave his name as "death to traitors, freedom for Britain".

There was a public outpouring of sympathy for Cox – a Go Fund Me crowd-funding appeal set up in her honour has raised more than £1.5 million. Campaigning in the referendum was formally suspended for two days and did not properly recommence until after the House of Commons, which was in recess and had to be recalled, paid tribute to Cox. Even after that, campaigning was somewhat more low-key than it had been. Cox, although only elected to the Commons in 2015, was well known and much liked by her parliamentary colleagues, not only on the Labour side. Gisela Stuart explained to us how the tragedy had emotional resonance to those on both sides of the referendum debate. Her killing brought home to others how vulnerable MPs are when they go about their work in their constituencies. Other MPs had been threatened during the tense atmosphere of the referendum campaign.

Most commentators assumed that the juxtaposition of a youngish female pro-Remain MP being murdered and the Brexiteers coming across as nasty would dissuade voters from backing Leave. It is far from clear that this is what happened. Polls did move towards Remain, but this movement appears to have begun before the Cox shooting. Referendums tend to move towards the status quo in their final stretch and the data suggests this had more to do with economic arguments. Cox's death and the suspension that followed threw the Remain camp off course, disrupting the campaign of last-minute alarmism they had been planning for the home stretch. In hindsight it does seem there was a notable lack of Remain figures telling voters "There's no going back if you vote Leave", a message with some potency.

UKIP had been planning to run a whole series of very strong ads on migration. The Breaking Point poster that Farage unveiled was described to us by one of those most responsible for it as entry level: "If it was Level One, we had posters ready to go which were Level Three." Cox's death meant these never saw the light of day. If Hannan is right in his assessment, the dumping of those posters will have boosted Leave.

A Brexit Tory MP with very different views on immigration to Hannan's more liberal stance also believes that the shooting had the opposite effect to that which most predicted. It meant that voters were thinking about immigration rather than economics in the last few days of the campaign – and immigration was an issue that played strongly for the Brexit cause.

Farage has few regrets about the Breaking Point poster, telling us: "The poster was a fact – a photograph that many newspapers had run on their front pages in 2015. And compared to the photos that the *Sun* and the *Mail* ran on their front pages before the referendum of refugees throwing stones at lorries in Calais, quite minor. The slogan 'The EU has failed us all' was a comment on what was going wrong. Was it a tough image? Of course it was. Was it designed to provoke debate? Of course it was. Had we thought about it very carefully? Of course we had. Did we know that 90 minutes after we launched it there was going to be a murder of an MP in the street? No. So the timing and the way in which it was used was deeply unfortunate."

How important was immigration to the Leave vote? Most of but not all the politicians we have spoken to – Hannan is a notable exception – say immigration was the issue most often raised on the doorstep. Michael Ashcroft conducted a large-scale survey of 12,300 people after they had voted: 49 per cent of Leave voters said their biggest single reason for wanting to leave the EU was "the principle that decisions about the UK should be taken in the UK". Coming second, 33 per cent said the main reason was that leaving "offered the best chance for the UK to regain control over immigration and its own borders". It was certainly a major reason for the Leave vote but perhaps not the predominant one. In any case, it is difficult to disentangle voters' motives, as a multiplicity of reasons will have played a part in their decisions.

Tellers count the votes on election night while Leave and Remain representatives watch.

Anthony Devlin/PA Wire/Press Association Images

Chapter Eight:
"We Took Back Control!"

Most Leave campaigners, from senior politicians to grassroots activists, spent the day of the referendum doing what they would have been doing had it been polling day in a general election: knocking on as many doors as possible, making sure their voters actually made it to the polling station.

Experienced campaigners will tell you that "knocking up", as this practice is known, can lull you into a false sense of security. You spend all day talking overwhelmingly to your own side and so any forecast as to the outcome of a vote based on anecdotes from the doorstep on polling day is worthless. Politicians may know this, but that does not mean they can stop themselves from trying to read the tea-leaves in the final stages of a long and draining campaign. Some of the Leave campaigners who spent 23 June talking to voters fell into this trap. Interviewed after the result, they described to us, variously, the positive mood, fantastic energy and encouraging signs on the day.

Most of the signs that day, however, pointed towards defeat for the Brexiteers. The polls published on the morning of the vote had Leave lagging behind Remain. Some predicted a wide margin of victory for the Prime Minister and Stronger In. Populus gave Remain a ten-point lead in its final poll, ComRes put it at eight points. Others were closer. IpsosMori and YouGov put the gap at four points and two points, respectively. As disconcerting as the polls was the behaviour of the markets. The pound rose 1.5 per cent to a six-month high against the dollar while the FTSE 100 reached a two-month high and stock markets across the continent also rose sharply. The message being sent was unambiguous: Brexit would not happen. Richard Tice described polling day as "really depressing". He said: "The night before, I thought it was really close but that we'd just do it. I was telling friends we would win by four or five per cent." Even if Tice could not understand why the collective wisdom of the market thought otherwise, he was disheartened nonetheless. He was not alone. Leave donors, politicians, and campaigners looked at the polls, the markets and the betting odds and thought the night was likely to end in disappointment.

Reports of queues at polling stations pointed to a high turnout, something which could be spun both ways by the Brexiteers. A low turnout would have been an unambiguously good thing for Leave, while a fairly high turnout suited Remain. But there was, according to some, a tipping point past which high turnout would actually suit Leave because it would mean segments of the electorate who do not normally vote had decided to do so in the referendum. Did the queues mean that turnout had passed that tipping point? As important as national turnout was the difference in turnout between different parts of the country. Optimistic Leavers were buoyed by the rain in London, where Remain expected to win by a comfortable margin. A suppressed turnout in the capital would certainly help, and when the rain grew heavier towards the end of the working day, the time most Londoners would vote, that started to look likely.

Gisela Stuart claims to have "given little thought to whether we'd win or lose". The Labour MP had grown used to nail-biting elections; holding her Edgbaston seat in Birmingham, which she won from the Conservatives in 1997, has consistently been a close-run thing and so she has learnt to concentrate on the task at hand rather than trying to predict the outcome. While she and Matthew Elliott travelled to the national centre for the referendum results in Manchester, neither Boris Johnson nor Michael Gove acted like men convinced they were about to win. The two most prominent Leave campaigners stayed in on the night of the vote. Gove went to bed early while Johnson stayed up and watched the results on television. Vote Leave would not hold a party that night – perhaps a sign that they were not exactly brimming with confidence.

Nigel Farage, however, would not avoid the public eye on referendum night. He was due to appear at Arron Banks's results party, which the Leave.EU founder was holding at the top of Millbank tower, where news cameramen, reporters and Leave activists milled about sipping Lord Ashcroft's English sparkling wine. A YouGov poll released as voting ended at 10pm – though not the more reliable sort of exit poll that predicts general election results – gave Remain a four-point victory. The UKIP leader released a statement to Sky News that appeared to concede defeat: "It's been an extraordinary referendum campaign, turnout looks to be exceptionally high, and looks like Remain will edge it. UKIP and I are going nowhere and the party will only continue to grow stronger in the future." With little to report on between the polls closing at 10 p.m. and the first counts declaring in the early hours of the next morning, much was made of this comment to fill the time. Soon afterwards, Farage arrived at Banks's party and, speaking from the middle of a media scrum, reiterated his fear that his side had lost, blaming the outcome on the extension of the deadline for voter registration by 48 hours after a government website crash. These comments reinforced the idea held by some of Farage's more strident opponents within the Leave camp that he was indeed hoping to lose as it might turbocharge support for UKIP in the same way that defeat in the Scottish referendum boosted the SNP. When we asked Farage whether defeat would have helped UKIP, he responded: "Massively. A narrow defeat and the Leave side saying the Prime Minister cheated – that would help UKIP. But that's not the point. I was thrilled to win."

Explaining his premature concession, Farage said he suffered "eleventh-hour nerves". Banks, who had seen private polling that predicted a Leave win, said he could not understand Farage's 10 p.m. statement. Those with the UKIP leader at the time were equally mystified. Farage and his team had gathered at the Westminster home of a UKIP campaigner. They were upbeat. They had seen the same polling as Banks and, Farage included, thought a Leave victory likely. When Farage went upstairs to get ready for the Banks party, the others were watching Sky News downstairs. They were surprised to see the presenter reporting comments from the man supposed to be shaving upstairs, and utterly that he appeared to be concede when he was, privately, optimistic.

Farage's talk of Brexit's demise was, as we now know, greatly overstated. When Newcastle voted Remain by a far narrower margin than most expected and then Sunderland voted Leave by a thumping 61 per cent to 39, the national trend pointed towards Brexit. Farage soon undid his concession speech, telling Leave.EU revellers: "Ladies and gentlemen, dare to dream that the dawn is breaking on an independent United Kingdom. If the predictions are right, this will be a victory for real people, a victory for ordinary people, a victory for decent people."

The exact moment of triumph inside the Vote Leave headquarters across the Thames came at around 4 a.m. when Dominic Cummings's fist broke through the ceiling above him, showering the Vote Leave campaign director in plaster as he stood on a desk and said to the assembled throng: "We did it. We bloody did it!" Moments earlier, Daniel Hannan had declared 23 June Independence Day before delivering what he calls a "garbled version" of the St Crispin's Day speech, made just before the Battle of Agincourt in *Henry V*:

This day is call'd the feast of Crispian.
He that outlives this day, and comes safe home,
Will stand a tip-toe when this day is nam'd,
And rouse him at the name of Crispian.
He that shall live this day, and see old age,
Will yearly on the vigil feast his neighbours,
And say "To-morrow is Saint Crispian."
Then will he strip his sleeve and show his scars,
And say "These wounds I had on Crispin's day."
Old men forget; yet all shall be forgot,
But he'll remember, with advantages,
What feats he did that day.

Britain voted to Leave by 52 per cent to 48.

Only a few hours later, standing in front of Number Ten, David Cameron announced his resignation, saying he thought the country needed "fresh leadership". He concluded: "Although leaving Europe was not the path I recommended, I am the first to praise our incredible strengths. I said before that Britain can survive outside the European Union and indeed that we could find a way. Now the decision has been made to leave, we need to find the best way and I will do everything I can to help. I love this country and I feel honoured to have served it and I will do everything I can to help this great country succeed."

***

In the days after victory, a message was sent to Vote Leave's entire email list. With its eccentric style and focus, it was impossible not to recognise it as the work of Dominic Cummings:

WE TOOK BACK CONTROL!

> Last week you changed the course of history. Vote Leave took on almost every force with power and money and we won. Britain chose to Vote Leave. This victory would not have happened without your amazing help and generosity. Thousands of you donated. Thousands of you volunteered. Thousands of you spoke to friends and family on our behalf to spread the message. THANK YOU!

> In just ten months we built from scratch an unprecedented national movement that took our campaign to every corner of

the country. We got to places that "politics as usual" ignored. People who have been ignored, and have never been involved in politics before, suddenly spoke out and took action.

In 2008, the worst financial crisis since 1929 hit the world. The people who paid the bill were mainly those on PAYE. They are still paying. They are also paying the bills for the EU's and the euro's dysfunction. Meanwhile many with power and money who were responsible for the mistakes and were completely wrong in their predictions dodged their fair share of the bills and got rich out of the EU system. We spoke for those on PAYE.

We did new things. Nobody in the UK has ever successfully built a web-based electoral database. Companies have spent millions and failed. We did it in a few months and succeeded. The combination of this database, our digital communication effort and our ground campaign broke new ground for political campaigns. This database product is worth a lot of money. We will shortly put the code online so that everyone can use it for free in the future (keep an eye on Github if interested). Hopefully it will help other campaigns give the public a powerful voice as we have. We've shown political parties how they can change and stop ignoring large parts of the country.

Why is this important? The British political system is broken in many ways and needs big changes – the EU is not our only problem. Our campaign was never controlled by any party though there were great people from all parties who helped us. All the parties have very deep problems. The way they are structured incentivises MPs to focus on themselves and their party – not the public interest.

It is important that the Conservative leadership candidates accept that the vote must be respected. Both the leading IN candidate (Theresa May) and the leading OUT candidate (Michael Gove) have made clear that if they win they will respect the vote and deliver a new UK-EU deal. This could mean, among other things, democratic control of immigration policy. This could marginalise extremists and allow a fair, sensible, and humane new policy. It could mean new trade deals and new jobs. It could mean more money for health, education, and science.

But we cannot be sure it will happen. In particular, while there are many wonderful civil servants there are also many who regard our victory as a disaster. They will try to stop or minimise changes. Not all the candidates in the Conservative leadership campaign have shown an ability to deliver big changes in the face of civil service opposition. Many in Labour are in complete denial about the real state of opinion and the real problems of the EU. Few MPs have the skills needed to manage normal government departments – never mind the EU negotiation and complex problems that implementing the referendum result require. Many MPs are desperate to ignore any lessons from the referendum and go back to politics as usual. The situation is very worrying.

Westminster cannot be relied upon. Taking back control to Britain is just the first step. The next step should be major political changes in Britain so that the broken Westminster and Whitehall system has to focus on the public interest in a way it does not now. If we increase the power of MPs and officials without changing how they behave, we will not solve our problems. We need organisations like Vote Leave to operate permanently to give a voice to those who otherwise won't be heard.

This campaign did not win because of support in Westminster – it won because of support in the country that has forced Westminster to listen. But three MPs in particular worked closely together and helped us win: Michael Gove (Conservative), Boris Johnson (Conservative), and Gisela Stuart (Labour) who was also a wonderful Chair. We want to thank all three of them too. They put their careers and reputations on the line. THANK YOU Boris, Gisela, and Michael. Thank you too to other MPs of all parties who helped, such as Anne-Marie Trevelyan and Graham Stringer.

It's been a privilege to have your support throughout this campaign. Your dedication brought victory.

On behalf of the team here at Vote Leave, and on behalf of the public, THANK YOU—and goodbye.

Best wishes

The Vote Leave HQ

P.S. If you want to keep in touch with events after we have won, then follow the private blog of our Campaign Director, Dominic Cummings. If we ever want to send up a "bat signal" that Westminster is cheating the vote and we need to form a new movement, you will see the bat signal there...

P.P.S. The website will remain online for many years. We are not using your data for any other purpose. All personal data will be permanently destroyed as we promised at the start. If you want to contribute to our "lessons learned" investigation, then please take this survey – CLICK HERE

It was not just Vote Leave staff congratulating themselves for what the email called an "unprecedented national movement". Elliott and Cummings, who had for months been the target for sniping from discontented Leave campaigners and the butt of jokes made by overconfident Remainers, were suddenly touted as giants of political campaigning. Writing in *The Times*, conservative journalist Tim Montgomerie argued that "the Vote Leave Campaign, led by Matthew Elliott and Dominic Cummings, was, with its 17,410,742 votes, the most successful political campaign in British history." In one sense this is true – more people voted for Brexit than have ever voted for anything else in the UK. But by Montgomerie's logic, Stronger In was the second most successful campaign in British history. We will never be able to say exactly how much credit Vote Leave deserves for delivering the Leave vote. It is hard to say with certainty how any campaign influences voters.

With some justice, the referendum was described as the most important vote that the electorate would cast in their lifetimes; it was much more significant than the result of any single general election. Yet the ground war on both sides was woeful compared to even the worst-run general election campaign for a major party.

In the ground war for a general election, parties canvass voters not to persuade them to change their minds (obviously if someone does so, it's a bonus) but to find out who their supporters are, and then to make sure they vote, be it by arranging postal ballots or by encouraging them to turn out on the day. Canvassing enables the major parties to build up a picture of their supporters over a number of elections.

The trouble for Vote Leave was that they did not have access to past Labour or Tory canvass returns nor to party workers. The exception to this was in seats where the sitting Tory MP was a Brexiteer. Virtually all local parties outside London overwhelmingly supported their MP and a traditional type of campaign could be fought. They were supported in this endeavour by Grassroots Out, Bone and Pursglove's organisation. These two MPs toured constituencies of pro-Brexit Tory MPs to rally their local activists and boost morale. In London the picture was rather different, with pro-Leave Tory MPs often being at odds with many of their constituency activists. While outside the capital for a Tory MP to support Leave would only shore up his constituency support, London MPs we have spoken to fear their pro-Brexit stance will cost them thousands of votes.

A traditional campaign could also be fought in Northern Irish seats held by the Democratic Unionist Party, which supported Leave as an entity. The ten Labour MPs who were publicly pro-Brexit were specifically not allowed to campaign in their own seats or to use the resources of their local party. Some deliberately avoided discussing the issue with their local activists in order to maintain constituency relations.

In spite of the fact that Leave-supporting Labour MPs' hands were tied, there does appear to have been a significant swing towards Brexit. On 17 April, an ICM poll put Labour support for Leave at 26 per cent. In the referendum itself, 37 per cent of Labour voters in the general election voted Leave. Some of the credit for that surely lies with Labour Leave, the organisation John Mills poured his efforts into after parting ways with Vote Leave in April. By 20 June, Labour Leave had 75,000 supporters signed up. It boasted an impressive social media presence, with more followers than the Labour In campaign, and vocalised the left-wing case for leaving the EU in a way those at Vote Leave and Leave.EU could not.

On the ground, Vote Leave did have enthusiastic UKIP members who were eager to help, but UKIP – as its few party apparatchiks will readily admit – has a terrible record at canvassing on its own behalf, with its activists not knowing the basics of the art. UKIP campaigners are much happier manning street stalls than knocking on doors. Vote Leave adopted the street stall approach – though without Cummings's added brainwave of charging those working on them for the privilege'.

Cummings, an Oxford history graduate, has a passionate enthusiasm for science writing, especially on matters of human diversity – an interest that some Vote Leave directors feared might be noticed and raised by the Remain side because of the racist connotations of debate on IQ – and astrophysics. The solution that he came up with to fill the gap for the campaign's lack of intelligence on the ground was to a hire a company employing astrophysicists who could use demographic data to predict where Leave voters would be found. The more data was fed into the system, the more reliable the results would be and the more precisely Leave voters could be targeted. This was obviously better than nothing – campaign insiders say it had a success rate of about 60 per cent. But it was a poor tool for getting the vote out – four in ten of those approached would either be non-voters or support the other side.

Vote Leave came up with another wheeze with which to identify potential supporters. The referendum coincided with the Euro 2016 football tournament in France. To highlight the cost of EU membership they decided to offer £50 million (the amount, according to Vote Leave's dubious maths, the UK sends to the EU every day) to whoever managed correctly to predict the outcome of every game in the tournament. Given that the chances of getting it right were staggeringly slim, Vote Leave were able to cover the potential payout by taking out insurance against anyone winning, a policy which reportedly cost £9,000. They spent roughly £200,000 developing the competition and its website and offered £50,000 to whoever correctly guessed the most consecutive results. Taking part cost voters nothing except their personal details and voting preferences. The Vote Leave campaigners who came up with this eccentric – and expensive – plan had high hopes, with some expecting as many as a million participants. Instead, the scheme was an unmitigated flop, with no more than 40,000 people registering. The sophistication of the messaging to those who did sign up appears to have been limited. One Leave-voting Islington resident received a text on polling day telling him "nearly everyone" in the neighbourhood was "with us". In reality just one in four Islington voters was on his side.

The Vote Leave board, presented with the football competition as a "fait accompli", according to one member, were unimpressed. One senior politician on the board called Cummings a "dangerous lunatic". Such a scheme hardly chimes with the post-victory claims of running the most sophisticated political campaign the country has seen.

Elliott's previous success in the campaign against AV seems to have led him and others involved in that campaign genuinely to believe that the brilliance of their efforts had turned British opinion around from being 60/40 per cent in favour of AV to rejecting it by 68/32 per cent – and that their talents could be employed in the EU referendum to bury the Remain side in a similar fashion. This is the purest piffle. The only polls which showed anything like a 60/40 majority for AV were held in the immediate aftermath of the Tory/Lib Dem coalition agreement when the new government, very much in its honeymoon period, had just announced that there would be a referendum on the voting system. Most polls were much more evenly balanced. More importantly, the vast majority of voters had no strong views on AV. Many would never have heard of it and others would have had only the vaguest notions of what it was. For this reason early polling on the subject would produce almost random results. Views on Europe were much more strongly held and would thus be much more difficult to shift, as indeed the 2016 referendum showed: there were no dramatic shifts in support. Some of those involved in both the AV and the Brexit campaigns were very disappointed by the final result, believing they could have pulled off something much more dramatic – a wholly misplaced feeling as such a shift was always very unlikely to happen. Just as opinions do not shift by 20 percentage points in a general election campaign – where much of the public has deep and long-held political affinities to one of the parties – they were not going to do so in the referendum. Elliott's AV campaign was not a masterclass in how to run a referendum – and the Vote Leave campaign most certainly was not.

Where Elliott has had notable success is as a fundraiser, most strikingly with the TaxPayers' Alliance, which he developed from a small group of recent LSE graduates, or more specifically LSE Hayek Society alumni, to the British campaigning organisation that probably gets more column inches than any other. The rules of the referendum meant that Vote Leave, as the lead campaign, could spend £7 million during the short campaign, starting on 15 April and going up to polling day. For some reason, these spending limits did not include staff costs or donations to other campaigning groups. These other groups – and there was no limit on how many there could be on either side, although there were restrictions on them acting in concert with each other – had to register with the Electoral Commission if they were going to spend more than £10,000 and could each spend up to £700,000. All donations over £7,500 given to a campaign after 1 February had to be declared to the Commission and were published, so it is easy to see who the major donors to the campaigns were.

Elliott did not have the advantages of either the official In campaign or of his Leave. EU rivals in having one dominant donor. David Sainsbury, the billionaire Labour peer and long-serving Blair-era science minister, who had previously been the last family member to be chairman of the eponymous supermarket chain, is very committed to the europhile cause and from February gave nearly £3 million to the official campaign from February. This was by no means the total extent of his support for the cause. Lord Sainsbury donated to both the Labour and Liberal Democrat campaigns for Remain. Those parties were allowed to spend up to £7 million and £3 million respectively; political parties which wished to campaign in the referendum had spending limits which depended on their share of the vote in the 2015 general election (the Conservatives opted out). Sainsbury gave each of them more than £2 million for their referendum campaigns. He also funded myriad other pro-Remain campaigns, including the European Movement, Scientists for EU, We are Europe, and Better for Our Future Ltd and Michelle Ovens Ltd. Perhaps Sainsbury's oddest donation was £210,000 to Virgin Management Ltd. In the immediate run up to the referendum Richard Branson decided to take out a series of advertisements in his own name to make the case for a Remain vote. The billionaire Branson was, however, less keen to pay for these ads so a donation from Sainsbury was solicited towards the cost. Arron Banks was willing to pour money into his Leave.EU vehicle. By his own reckoning he spent £6.5 million on Leave.EU, although some of this was in the form of loans, and he also backed UKIP and other pro-Brexit campaigns.

The battle for designation made fundraising much more tricky for Elliott. Many potential donors would not commit until they knew who would lead the campaign. The first donor – and overall largest, to Vote Leave was Jeremy Hosking, investor and railway enthusiast: he gave £915,000 during the designated period and about £250,000 before that. Hosking was approached by Bernard Jenkin and agreed to give the campaign a donation of £50,000 before it had even set up a bank account. In the hope of combining his interest in Brexit and steam trains, Hosking came up with the idea of running one of his trains around the country with Leave campaigners giving stump speeches off the back of it. While he acknowledges the scheme could have generated adverse headlines – Back to the Steam Age, and so on – he thought its eccentricity would appeal to the British public. Boris Johnson was apparently enthusiastic and Elliott initially suggested that it was a runner, but eventually the idea was rejected. Hosking set up his own campaign, Brexit Express, although it never used a train either; instead, it spent £626,000 on a billboard advertising campaign.

Vote Leave managed to raise more than it was allowed to spend, but it fell back heavily on the "usual suspects" of Euroscepticism. Patrick Barbour committed to giving £1 million, but after donating an initial £500,000 had misgivings about the direction of the campaign and the use of the £350 million figure; instead, he supported other parts of the Brexit movement. Stuart Wheeler donated more than £600,000; International Motors, the company of Robert Edmiston, Conservative peer and longstanding Eurosceptic donor, gave £850,000 during the designated period. This was the second-largest single donation to Vote Leave.

The largest single donation received by Vote Leave came as a surprise to the campaign. Diana Van Nievelt Price, who in 2005 had given the Conservatives £440,000 when she bought a portrait of Margaret Thatcher at a charity auction, telephoned Vote Leave and said she had decided to make a donation of £1 million. The campaign was sceptical, asking her to first make a donation of £1,000 via the website. Only once she had thus proved her credentials were moves set afoot to secure her pledge.

Donations totalling £600,000 by Gladys Bramall, an 87-year-old widow from Sutton Coldfield who owned a construction plant hire business with her late husband, became an issue for Vote Leave when it was revealed that her name had been found on a leaked 2006 membership list of the racist British National Party. Mrs Bramall was unaware that she had been a member, apparently having been signed on by her late husband without her knowledge. Considering that Mrs Bramall was one of the largest donors to Vote Leave, the fact that this news, which could easily be discovered via a Google search of her name, as the old BNP membership lists had been posted on the Web, came as a surprise to Vote Leave suggests that their due diligence was not as rigorous as it might have been.

While the Leave side feared that they might be heavily outspent in the referendum, as they had been in 1975, when the official Yes campaign outspent the No campaign eleven-fold, and if unofficial spending is included by up to twenty-fold, the two sides were in reality fairly equally matched. Before purdah kicked in, the Remain side was certainly at a financial advantage because of the use of government resources, but after that the Leave side was, if anything, at a slight advantage. It does not say much for the number of people in Britain who have a deep commitment to European integration that they were so reliant on the largesse of Sainsbury.

Perhaps the oddest donations in the whole campaign were not to Vote Leave but from it. The campaign raised more money than it was allowed to spend itself, so made various donations to other campaigners. There were three recipients: Muslims for Britain received £10,000, Labour Leave – as a parting gift – £15,000, and Darren Grimes, a 23-year-old libertarian design student at Brighton, £625,000. Grimes headed BeLeave, aimed at millennials, which ran a social media campaign. Apparently Grimes had accidentally registered himself, rather than BeLeave, as the referendum participant and hence donations were given to him rather than his campaign. The Vote Leave board as a whole were unaware of the donations to Grimes – there were three – but such matters were under the supervision of a subsidiary committee. Elliott has insisted to us that none of the money was paid to Grimes directly and it all went to an advertising agency. The donations were, however, declared as "cash" to the Electoral Commission; payments to third parties such as advertising agencies should be declared as "non-cash". Grimes went on to work for Brexit Central, the site set up by Elliott to monitor progress on the UK's extraction from the EU.

In the months and years to come, there will inevitably be much haggling over the legacy of the referendum. Whenever you hear someone claiming credit for the result – and there is already a wide cast of characters doing so – remember that no one individual, organisation or party delivered the Leave vote. Neither Dominic Cummings's campaigning genius, nor Nigel Farage's charisma, nor Matthew Elliott's fundraising prowess, nor Arron Banks's straight-talking singlehandedly brought about the result they all fought for. The Brexit movement was a messy, incoherent phenomenon that veered from being its own worst enemy to working as a potent political force with popular appeal. In the end, of course, it got what it wanted – but the credit for that must ultimately go to the British people. 🎔

Appendix:
The Results

Region (Number of valid votes)	Remain	Leave	Turnout
England (28,455,547)	46.6	53.4	73
East (3,328,983)	43.5	56.5	75.7
East Midlands (2,508,515)	41.2	58.8	74.2
London (3,776,751)	59.9	40.1	69.7
North East (1,340,698)	42	58	69.3
North West (3,665,945)	46.3	53.7	70
South East (4,959,683)	48.2	51.8	76.8
South West (3,172,730)	47.4	52.6	76.7
West Midlands (2,962,862)	40.7	59.3	72
Yorkshire and The Humber (2,739,235)	42.3	57.7	70.7
Northern Ireland (790,149)	55.8	44.2	62.7
Scotland (2,679,513)	62	38	67.2
Wales (1,626,919)	47.5	52.5	71.7
Total (33,577,342)	48.1	51.9	72.2